WHEN SLEEP COMES

Shillelagh Songs

JACK FOLEY

Sagging
Meniscus

Some of these poems appeared in *Poetry Flash*, for which I am grateful. For the most part, the poems in this book are recent and previously unpublished. The opening paragraph of my Author's Introduction appears as the opening paragraph of my review of Michael McClure's *Persian Pony*; it was published in *Beat Scene* (Number 91, Winter 2018). The Ferlinghetti poem was published in my collaboration with Helen Breger, *Sketches Poetical* (2012); "Sea Breeze" appears in my selected poems, *EYES* (2013), as do some of the lines from "Artaud." The photos on pages 54, 58, and 121 were taken by me. The photo on page 56 was taken by Nurulwahida Jamaludin; the photo on page 129 was taken by Kerry Foley.

Printed in the United States of America.
Set in Adobe Garamond with LaTeX.

ISBN: 978-1-944697-86-0 (paperback)
Library of Congress Control Number: 2019951546

Sagging Meniscus Press
Montclair, New Jersey
www.saggingmeniscus.com

To Sangye, Sean, Kerry, Ivan, Jake,
Joe, Dana, Carl, Jacob, Al, Nina, Paul,
and to the memory of so many, especially Adelle

Vogon poetry is of course the third worst in the Universe. The second worst is that of the Azgoths of Kria. During a recitation by their Poet Master Grunthos the Flatulent of his poem "Ode to a Small Lump of Green Putty I Found in My Armpit One Midsummer Morning" four of his audience died of internal hemorrhaging, and the President of the Mid-Galactic Arts Nobbling Council survived by gnawing one of his own legs off. Grunthos is reported to have been "disappointed" by the poem's reception . . .

Douglas Adams, *The Hitchhiker's Guide to the Galaxy*

It can only be the thought of verdure to come, which prompts us in the autumn to buy these dormant white lumps of vegetable matter covered by a brown papery skin, and lovingly to plant them and care for them. It is a marvel to me that under this cover they are labouring unseen at such a rate within to give us the sudden awesome beauty of spring flowering bulbs. While winter reigns the earth reposes but these colourless green ideas sleep furiously.

C.M. Street, responding to Noam Chomsky's famous sentence

The sandwich store was popular and very busy. Sandwiches were made from scratch. On this day, there was a long line of patient, expectant people. A young woman ordered three complicated sandwiches. She said to the server, "While you make my sandwiches, I'm going to read you some of my poetry." She pulled out a notebook and began to read. The person who told me this story explained that the woman's poems were all about her mother. She "hated" her mother. He added, "You're probably acquainted with this woman."

Jack Foley, "The Sandwich Store"

We are angels of reading

We read
the book of the blue sky
which masks
the blackness
and infinity
of "space"
our home is with the infinite, no?

Jack Foley, "Requiem"

He has come back to the place where he grew up as a monk. The message is to remember we don't come from nowhere. We have roots. We have ancestors. We are part of a lineage or stream. It's a beautiful message, to see ourselves as a stream, as a lineage, and it is the deepest teaching in Buddhism: non-self. We are empty of a separate self, and yet at the same time, we are full of our ancestors . . . [Thich Nhat Hanh] is alive in my breath, in my awareness.

Brother Phap Dung on Thich Nhat Hanh

Shillelagh law was all the rage.

"Finnegan's Wake"

Contents

WHEN SLEEP COMES   161

APPENDIX   167

AFTERWORD & NOTES   175

WHEN SLEEP COMES

AUTHOR'S INTRODUCTION

In his great poem, "Out of the Cradle Endlessly Rocking" (1859), Walt Whitman constantly seeks a name for the kind of language he has invented for his complex, multi-voiced, multi-selved poem, resonating with echoes from the Bible (particularly the Psalms), from the highly theatrical opera of his day—the notion of the "aria" is central to the piece—even from the world of the newspaper, which was one of the places in which Whitman developed his understanding of writing. The term he chooses for this language, which is alive with the notion of performance, is not verse or poetry or prose or prose poetry—the term "free verse" was not available to him—but *song*. This notion of *song* was a redefinition of the possibilities of language in a specifically American context. In his extraordinary essay, "Projective Verse" (1950), Charles Olson extends Whitman's insights into techniques partially gleaned from the French Symbolist movement, in which the silence and whiteness of the page is not neutral but an active element in the meaning of what the poet intends. In addition, breath—the breathing of syllables—becomes a central issue in the enunciation of the work. Together, Whitman and Olson—with, no doubt, some help from William Carlos Williams, among others—give living poets, and particularly American poets, a medium in which they can find their own erratic, imaginative way.

WHITMAN'S "OUT OF THE CRADLE ENDLESSLY ROCKING"

(EXPOESIS)

I don't think there is another *poem*
More unique
And, simultaneously,
More representative of
What we may call the American spirit
Than this amazing
Presentation of the making of a poet
Of the transformation of anyone
From childhood to a condition of knowledge
How do we enter the world in a deep way
It is an aria, a performance
Something Whitman saw in the opera houses,
It is a multi-voiced, multi-selved poem in which
All sorts of styles and "voices" are brought together
(Including the hissing voice of the old crone, the sea, and the voice of
the bird, "my dusky demon and brother," "the lone singer wonderful")
It is a poem about family (the he-bird, the she-bird)
It is a poem about the stunning fact of Death the Opener
And the great representation of the sea (Melville)
(The sea is the openness of consciousness)
It is a nature poem
In which the "outsetting bard" merges with what he sees
It includes Quakers ("Ninth-month midnight")
And Native Americans ("Paumanok")
It is Whitman giving himself over to the sheer possibilities of music
As world becomes word ("translating")
It is an act of marvelous empathy and compassion in the literal sense,
"feeling with"
It is a poem about the body and its transformation
Even as Whitman speaks of the soul
It is a poem in which the lorn bird and the transforming boy
Move us to what Wallace Stevens called
A new representation of reality.
This, camerados, is the great mythic moment of American letters
And it takes place not at a desk but outside,
Not as writing but as brilliant spontaneous unexpected utterance.
It ushers in (under the magical multivalent moon, in the presence of the
vast, talkative
sea)
Nothing less than the world as song.

SHILLELAGH

"Cudgel," 1772, earlier, "oak wood used to make cudgels" (1670s), from *Shillelagh*, town and barony, famous for its oaks, in County Wicklow, Ireland. The name is literally "seeds" (or descendants) of *Elach*, from Irish *síol* "seed."*

Here in Oakland
Far from Shillelagh
I sing some songs
From the new world—
Seeds (*síol*)

Remembering the
Old

*www.etymonline.com

THE WINGS,
THE RIVER,
THE WIND

THE WINGS THE RIVER THE WIND

the strangeness of ashes
that hold nothing but memory
what's left of the dear thing
whose hand you once held
and who held yours
the strangeness
that what had been so solid
and lodged in the heart
should vanish
this is the word "evanescence"
these are the wings, the river, the wind

ANGELOS

I have always wanted to believe
In angels, always looked for
Traces of their wings,
Their beauty and swiftness,
Birds and humans, "messengers"
Especially the guardians
Those assigned particularly to you
How lovely to have an invisible friend
Who looks after you and moves you
Just an inch
When the brick heading directly for your head
Is about to fall.

I have always wanted to believe
In angels and do at some level.
Do you know the word "eudemonia"?
It means happiness but is by etymology
"Good demons, good spirits."
Angels are such.

The man who asked me for money
Yesterday
But who looked at me with such searching intensity
As if we shared a secret
Was perhaps my "good demon"

For, according to ancient doctrine,
Demons too do the work of God.

Demons too do the work of God.
For, according to ancient doctrine,

Was perhaps my "good demon"
As if we shared a secret
But who looked at me with such searching intensity
Yesterday
The man who asked me for money

Angels are such.
"Good demons, good spirits."
It means happiness but is by etymology
Do you know the word "eudemonia"?
In angels and do at some level.
I have always wanted to believe

Is about to fall.

When the brick heading directly for your head
Just an inch
Who looks after you and moves you
How lovely to have an invisible friend
Those assigned particularly to you
Especially the "guardians"
Birds and humans, "messengers"
Their beauty and swiftness
Traces of their wings,
In angels, always looked for
I have always wanted to believe

BY PERSIS KARIM:

Ask the river anything
and the answer will always
be the same: *give me water.*

I cannot bear to be
a river that does not live
up to its name.

JACK'S ANSWER:

Ask the river anything
    riverrun, past Eve and Adam's,
and the answer will always
    from swerve of shore to bend of bay,
be the same: *give me water*
    brings us by a commodious vicus of

I cannot bear to be
    recirculation back. . .
a river that does not live
    you are a river, Persis,
up to its name
    full of the multitudes a river carries

FOR CHIP DEFFAA

Speak to the dead though they do not hear
Speak to the dead though they do not hear
Speak to the dead though they will not answer
Speak to the dead though they will not answer
Speak to the dead for they are near
Speak to the dead for they are near
Nearer than you believe
Nearer than you believe
In their graves in the ground
In their graves in the ground
Or their ashes;
Or their ashes;
Speak to them for they are pure spirit now
Speak to them for they are pure spirit now
And no longer need your love or approbation or anyone's care
And no longer need your love or approbation or anyone's care
Speak to them for they are like angels
Speak to them for they are like angels
Their faces shining with non existence
Their faces shining with non existence
They are naked like angels
They are naked like angels
They too have wings
They too have wings
They smile in a way that is pure enigma
They smile in a way that is pure enigma
More baffling than *La Gioconda*
More baffling than La Gioconda
They are beyond suffering, joy, and the sorrows of love
They are beyond suffering, joy, and the sorrows of love
They chime like the Balangiga bells
They chime like the Balangiga bells
They knock at the door of your heart and demand that you answer
They knock at the door of your heart and demand that you answer

ELEGY: GOODBYE, BEAT THING

Beat ephemera
Beat lounge acts
Beat cruise
Beat correspondence
Beat fairs
Beat things

Beat wax museums
Beat food
Beat—

War Won Ton
Edsel Fong
Flamenco

Blaze against cement
Geeks cling to

Claghorn's the name
Down the block from Bebop
"Ornithology"
Evaporate mouth tongue ocean fun

Weetles and blorks

Nuclear August 13th rain of ruin
After two more jolts Ethel Rosenberg
Met her maker

"GENE TIERNEY'S ORDEAL"
. . .

He
Could no longer speak
But his eyes
Spoke
He smiled
Alive
For only a brief time now
I do not know
What darkness he entered
Words he made
Stay with me
I told him,
You laid it down,
We got to
Pick it up

    for David Meltzer

ELEGY: TEARS FOR JEFFREY LILLY

Another death
In my life
Another good man
Gone
So sorry to hear of it,
Jeffrey
A wonderful Jewish man
Given to laughter
And tears
Had it been I
Instead of you
I'm sure you would have had some words.
That I am speaking such words here
Is purely a question of Chance
And Luck.
Dear man,
I remember your smile
And your deep awareness:
There is no contradiction
Between being Jewish
And being gay.
There is no contradiction
Between being Jewish
And being gay.
To be gay
Is simply to be human.
You were always for me,
My friend,
And I am for you here
In whatever place,
Whatever Sheol
Whatever Olam Ha-Ba
You enter now

"Do not be as ones who labor for their master mindful of the reward that will be
        coming, but
rather as those who serve their master with love and with joy"

So it was with you
Shalom
    Shalom

ART CRAZY: LEONARD BREGER

The most vivid of men
His great bulk now
      Lying prone on a bed
Across from his great self-portrait
      Breger as dragon
Leonard, I wished
      You could paint what I saw:
The great man failing
      But the image of him
In full power
      Denying everything registered by my eyes.
Tears.
      You looked at me
With your marvelous eyes
      But I don't know whether
You recognized me.
      Lift me, you commanded.
And held your hands out
      I tried.
Lift me.
      Where were my powers?
Couldn't raise you.
All I could do
      Was hold you,
Briefly,
      In a moment
As clouds flew
      Across your room—
High up
      Where you will be
Forever and forever and forever.

Forever and forever and forever.

FIRE BRICKS

for two voices

These bricks have been through a fire
    These bricks have been through a fire
That is different from the fire
    That is different from the fire
All bricks go through:
    All bricks go through
They tell a story
    They tell a story
Of something that happened
    Of something that happened
More than a hundred years ago
    More than a hundred years ago
They are speech—their misshapen, crude
    They are speech—their misshapen, crude
Violent bodies are mouths
    Violent bodies are mouths
Crying out the Lamentation of 1906
    Crying out the Lamentation of 1906
"one of the worst natural disasters in the history of the United States"
    "one of the worst natural disasters in the history of the United States"
They are frozen permanent mouths
    They are frozen permanent mouths
That say, Aie Aie
    That say, Aie Aie
Memorials to horror
    Memorials to horror
And yet:
    And yet:
Re-used . . . Stranger,
    Re-used . . . Stranger,
Live in this building and know
    Live in this building and know
What the flames
    What the flames
Could twist
    Could twist
And turn to the unutterable
    And turn to the unutterable
To shapes of endless pain
    To shapes of endless pain
And suffering
    And suffering

But
> *But*

Could not
> *Could not*

(Finally)
> *(Finally)*

Kill.
> *Kill.*

REFLECTIONS AFTER A FUNERAL

As the formalists die, so do the free versifiers
As the beats perish, so do the squares
    Borges—John would have known it—
As the soloists go, so do the quires,
We all go up or down the stairs
    said each of us runs the risk
To heaven, as in the Powell-Pressburger film
Whose hero is a poet. As I go, so do you.
    of being the first immortal.
We live until life stops us. Flam-
Boyant death traps us in the loo,
    Small risk. John knew that too.
In bed, while driving our fancy automated automobile,
In Georgia, Idaho, Alabama, Kalamazoo,
    We live till life stops us.
San Francisco, New York, Natchez, Mobile,
Philadelphia, with a girl in Saint Lou—
    Words—palabras—
Formal, free (Walla Walla) into the forsaken dark
Aflame in San Diego, alive in Luna Park.
    save us (we hope)

    for John Oliver Simon

LAWRENCE FERLINGHETTI, PRIDE OF YONKERS, NY, TURNS 100 ON MARCH 24, 2019

My name was Lawrence Ferling.
There are more allusions in my poetry
than there are in *The Waste Land*.
I am a painter and a publisher and a book
store owner. After
invading Normandy,
I came to San Francisco.
I published one of the greatest dirty poems of the twentieth century.
I took the phrase "a coney island of the mind"
from Henry Miller and made it
the title of my marvelous, hugely popular book of poems.
Like Jack Kerouac, I spoke French to my mother
except (but I didn't know) she was my aunt.
I had an incredibly complex, confusing childhood
but was nonetheless a child of privilege.
I wrote painterly poems and "oral messages."
I embraced the downtrodden, the lost, the outcast.
I denounced the government and "autogeddon"
(a word I took from Heathcote Williams)
but was a successful and eventually rich
businessman
My bookstore became a national monument.
I am a street in the city of San Francisco.
Vorrei ringraziare tutti—e anche i miei genitori immigranti.
I am Lawrence
Ferlinghetti.
I never knew my father.

DEATH LOVES POETS

JACK: Death likes poets. IVAN: Death just Loves Poets, the more the better!!!
You and I tread steps and walks made of wind! Don't take much for a fatal misstep!

There, another one—Death loves poets
John Oliver Simon—another one
Julia Vinograd—Death loves poets
Peter Sherburn-Zimmer—there, still another—Jeffrey Lilly
"Steps and walks made of wind"
And what of Larry Eigner, James Broughton, Maya Angelou, Ntozake Shange,
What of David Bromige, Lynn Lonidier, Robert Duncan, David Antin, Philomene
    Long,
Leslie Scalapino, David Lerner, Joie Cook, Jack Micheline, Donald Schenker,
Denise Levertov, Marsha Getzler, David Meltzer, Stanley McNail, my wife Adelle,
Carolyn Kizer, Chana Bloch, Phil Whalen, Harold Norse, Allen Ginsberg, Lou
    Harrison,
Paul Mariah, Adrienne Rich, Tom Clark, Ron Loewinsohn, James Schevill, Jack
    Mueller,
    so many,
You can be sure Death whispers sweet nothings in their ears
Until they *are* sweet nothings
Which one will be next? Al Young is in the hospital with "a major stroke"
May the ravenous bastard keep his hands off Al!
Even though Al is a wonderful poet and Death must love and want him
Because Death loves poets but sometimes lets them live a little (Lawrence
    Ferlinghetti)
We get in the habit
Of saying certain things
Presenting ourselves in certain ways
Until the Angelic Wind blows that apart
We love certain people
Think of them with kindness and affection
Until the Angelic Wind blows that apart
Is Death an Angelic Wind
We might as well call it a Diabolical Wind
It doesn't matter
It's a force that blows something apart
Something we thought solid and immutable
Until the Diabolical-Angelic
The Angelic-Diabolical
Insists that we were wrong.
We exist
Not as rocks or trees or garages
We are waves of the sea
Shape-shifting at the will
Of something we will never know

At one moment, one thing
At another, another
And telling ourselves
(Until the Angelic Wind reminds us)
That we are constant
That we are unities
Not the leaves
Not the scraps of wind-blown paper
Not the flower petals
That
We are

YEARS POEM

An old friend, Tom Hanna, whom I hadn't heard from in some years, showed up on Facebook. We had been young poets at Cornell. I proposed the questions that are the title of this poem.

WHAT HAVE THE YEARS BROUGHT TO YOU?
WHAT HAVE THEY TAKEN AWAY?

BROUGHT

Adelle / Sangye
Sangye / Adelle
Sean, and through Sean, Kerry.
A lifetime long enough
To watch my son grow
Into an intelligent, interesting adult
Poetry, art, music,
The movies,
Plays.
Friends.
Poetry above all.
A lifetime long enough
A marriage—
But also a death
"Grief, thief of time"
A lifetime long enough to "be" someone
To accumulate knowledge that
Feeds upon the knowledge I came to
As a young man
The sudden awareness at 15
Of another possibility of consciousness
The awareness at 78
That that very possibility is granted by the nature of "language"
(Tongue's telling)
Ithaca
California
Chapel of the Chimes
Appearance on *The Ed Sullivan Show* (1955)
The ability to remember
And the ability to fictionalize
The ability to draw
Radical intelligence
Orgone Boxes
Television
Books

Musicals
Computers
My cell phone
The Golden Age of Radio
Sagging Meniscus Press
Story
Charles Olson
James Joyce
Gertrude Stein
Chaucer
Shakespeare
De Quincey
Shelley
Coleridge
Auden
Frost
Poe
Hawthorne
Wordsworth
Artaud ('TO END GOD'S JUDGMENT")
Thomas Gray ("Had he written often thus"—world opening at 15 years)
Hughes ("De Bop")
Mina Loy
Marianne Moore
H.D.
David Bromige ("One Spring")
Kenneth Rexroth (the angry king)
D.H. Lawrence
Jack Teagarden
Ziggy Elman's solo on "And the Angels Sing"
Cole Porter
Whitman ("Out of the Cradle")
Melville
Hegel
Robert Duncan
Dylan Thomas
Baudelaire
Catullus
Virgil
Homer
Sappho of Lesbos
Jelly Roll Morton
Hart Crane
Duke Ellington
Fats Waller
Mallarmé

Charles Ives
And Charles Ives again
(*The Concord Sonata*!)
Walter J. Ong
Napoléon vu par Abel Gance
Early Disney
The guitar
Gene Kelly
The possibility of loving my mother
Despite her madness
My father dapper in his tie and suit
And in his underwear
Solitaire
Bach
Beethovan
Alfred Hitchcock
Larry Eigner
James Broughton
Dana Gioia
Dave Mason
Sciatica
The Nicolas Brothers
The capacity for compassion
The disagreement
With every priest
Who has tried to convince me
Of his holiness
The Holy—
Radiance
Light
Darkness
Women
Men
Circumstance
Persons are not holy,
Experiences are (or may be)
The magnificent stars
Ash from the fires
That burn near
But not too near
Rain
Tap dancing
Stairs
Fruit
Fred Astaire
Pho for my delight

Pasta
Ice Cream
Paul de Man
The notion of
Blindness & Insight
Heidegger—life changer
The bosom of
My love
Pillows
Cassettes
CDs
Automobiles
And the ability to drive them
Words that spring
From unknown sources
Unknown sources
Wind
Dust
The sky
Air
The wild birds
My goldfish
My house
Phonograph records
Computers
Fingers
Toes
Knees
Thighs
Sex
Kisses
Hugs
Dellwackians
"The Monst"
Ice Cream sodas
(Still a tradition in Alabama)
Irving Berlin
George Gershwin
Georges Brassens
Rilke
(*Du mußt dein Leben ändern*)
Eliot, Pound, the radio
KPFA
Erik Bauersfeld
Susan Stone
Jess

Ishmael Reed
Al Young
The ability to make a list like this
Which is only partial
Death
Diabetes
Money
Great sorrow
Great joy
"It's karma, baby"
Openness
Sweetness of infants
Frankentrump
Yeats
Dante
The young
Thought
French
German
Latin
Sanskrit
Spanish—all its dialects
Italian—all its dialects
Arabic
Catalan
American linguistic innocence
THE CATHOLIC CHURCH
Syria, "before"
(The beautiful young people there)
Old friends
Who show up
On Facebook
Facebook
My Italian
Relatives
Birthdays
Vaudeville
Mangos
Adelle / Sangye
Sangye / Adelle
Sean, and through Sean, Kerry.
. . .
The Beatles
"Jack Foley Day" in Berkeley (June 2010)
Two Lifetime Achievement Awards
Eddie Lang

Les Paul
The Golden Gate Quartet
Magic (and Magick)
The Tarot (especially Crowley's)
"The Tarzan Tree"
The Supremes
Hugger Mugger in the Louvre
Tolkien (reading from *The Hobbit*)
A wonderful production of *Under Milk Wood*
At Cornell University ca. 1960
Richard Fariña in it
(Fariña dead at 29!)
D.H. Lawrence
("Not I, not I, but the wind that blows through me")
John Crowe Ransom (beautiful appearance at Cornell)
Lewis Rubman (best man, lost friend)
Pablo Picasso
Max Ernst
Dorothea Tanning
The Wizard of Oz
Laurel & Hardy
Roy Rogers ("My Chickashay Gal")
Gene Autry (the serial, *The Phantom Empire*)
Flash Gordon (the serial, the great newspaper comic)
COMIC BOOKS
The Shadow
Captain Midnight
"The Secret Squadron"
The decoder ring and arrowhead
The Lone Ranger (I shamed my father by watching it on a friend's TV:
Father responded by buying a TV)
Brace Beemer
Cathy Lewis
Fred Allen (*Treadmill to Oblivion*)
Our Miss Brooks
Charlie McCarthy
E.E. Cummings
Lead Belly
James Joyce's amazing recording ("Well you know . . ..")
Tears
Some Like It Hot
Fritz Lang
Dalí
Breton
Corinne Heline (*The Moon in Occult Lore*)
Leonard Breger (portrait)

Anthony Holdsworth (portrait)
The Way of All Flesh
Bernard Shaw—liberating, liberating, liberating
Hart Crane
Lao Tse
Jesus
Louis Zukofsky
Homophonia
Evelyn Waugh
("Ain't gonna study Waugh no more")
C.S. Lewis (the trilogy)
The need
To experience
Depth
Country Joe and the Fish
Pete Seeger
Woody Guthrie
Houdini
Movie stars
William Blake
Alba Cosenza
Joe Masi
Mary-Marcia Casoly
Clara Hsu
Betsy Davids
Jake Berry
Bridget Berry
Chris Mansel
Ceil Tanner
Bob Tanner
Wayne Sides (and the KKK!)
Rose Ray
Tommy Lagonia (beautiful, young, short-lived, unremembered)
Mike Lurie (dead long years ago—"My parents were psychiatrists. When they criti-
    cized me, they were RIGHT")
Ed Mycue
Diane di Prima
Gerald Vizenor
Julia Vinograd
Diamond Dave
Frank De Giacomo
Louis De Giacomo
Their mother and father (still remembered)
My uncle Panny ("automobile beautician")
Aunt Maggie (of unparalleled enormity, "it's her glands")
Cousin Richie

Carlota Caufield
Richard Segasture
Judy
Dave & Gail Boesel
Steve Kaplan, first of the dead in my reckoning
Mike Lurie
Red Ryder and Little Beaver
Sinatra
Ray Charles
Nick Tosches
McClure
Rothenberg
Ginsberg
Welles
Bazin
Keaton
Kaufman
Ted Jones
Chaplin
John Milton
Milton Berle
Jack Benny
Freud
Jung
Reich
"Revision is addition, not subtraction"
The perception
That *some parts of the mind*
Don't know
What other parts of the mind
Are doing
Buddhism
Existentialism
Sartre
De Beauvoir
Lorca ("sad wind among the olive trees")
George M. Cohan
Noël Coward
Tom Jones
Warren Wechsler
Thomas Wolfe (*Look Homeward, Angel*! "A wind is rising . . ..")
Cocteau (*The Blood of a Poet, Orpheus, Thomas the Imposter,*
Chappelle in Milly-la-Forêt)
"The Angel Heurtebise"
Argüelles (umlaut ablaze!)
Bill Allen (thanks for the teachings!)

Billie Holiday
Louis Armstrong
Ella Fitzgerald
Rodgers & Hart
My aunt Goldie, Ziegfeld girl
My old tap shoes
Gale Prawda, cuz
Ravi Prawda (Ravi Ravissimo!)
Robin Ann Nicholas
Felicia Twardy
Stanley McNail, poet of horror
Helen Adam, poet of horror
Witches
Dragon Rouge
"Forms, measured forms"
The need to discover
New forms
If new forms may ever be said
To be discovered
Mary Rudge
Nina Serrano
Mario Savio
Paul Veres
Carl Landauer
Michael Lerner
Tony Perez and his songs
My son's new book—
Occasion of joy that it came and
Tears, that his mother couldn't see it
Saudi Arabia
Paris
Kuala Lumpur
Australia
Mexico
Canada
The Free Speech Movement
The realization that I am capable of hatred,
That there are some things I cannot or will not
Forgive—despite my commitment to
Compassion and Forgiveness—
Some things that cause anger
To rise up in me again and again
As in its first fury.
Compassion and Forgiveness
Edouard Muller
Kriska

Comment ça va, petit? (Michael)
Rape, murder
Kitka
Guillermo Galindo
Was, der Herr hat keine Moneten?
Was, der Herr will nicht bezahlen?
Wissen Sie, was das bedeutet?
At 21 I saw it:
Brecht: not self expression: dialectics
The phantoms who haunt me, whose names I have forgotten
The Maltese Falcon ("gunsel")
Teriolo
"Philadelphoo"
Port Chester
Berkeley
New York
Oakland
Nashville
The loneliest bus stop in the world, Scranton, Pennsylvania
Florence, Alabama
Perth Amboy
Neptune (where first I breathed the air)

TAKEN AWAY

Adelle, Adelle foremost, Adelle and again, Adelle
Hoppinjohn, meat sauce, beignets, fruit cakes
Foods that bring tears
Because she made them
Her haiku, written on anything
Scraps of newspaper, anything
Her conversation
Strands of my hair that used to flower
The ease of walking (the gift of sciatica)
My old tap shoes
Thinness
Ability to fit into certain clothes
Ability to wash dishes or brush teeth without tiring
Ability to get through a day without a nap
Ability to read a boring book without falling asleep
Friendship, even love, of certain people.
And now, watching it, John Fitzgerald Kennedy's
Eulogy
For Robert Frost
Brings tears.
John Fitzgerald Kennedy's

Eulogy
For Robert Frost
Displays clearly
All *we* have lost
Kennedy's Eulogy
Is Praise
Of the poetic impulse
(Which, for him, is not separate from the political impulse)
It tears
At the heart of our lost nation
What dark truths do we live among now
Since these men died?
What city
Shines now
Upon a hill?
The abundance
Of dear friends
Who have died:
A hill of death and loss
I carry on my shoulders
(Larry Eigner's
Impossible to understand
Patois
On the phone)
Words
I have forgotten
My own and others'
Faces
I no longer recognize
Though once
They shone
In my consciousness
What was his name?
What was hers?
What was the name
Of that song
I almost remember?
I come upon these lines
From a poem I wrote
Long years ago
Could I have written them now?
blond hair
    has certain privileges
        but it grays
sooner than most—
    I see you

at the store
  on the street
    at the poetry
      reading
and think: your hands your eyes your
      body
might have had
  a different cast—
Are we
  unhappy? Do we want
this,
  another,
    or perhaps a third?
I read
  the book,
   a book
of names
  and places—
yours:
  "eudemonia" ("happiness")—
    "benevolent
      demons"—
& think:
  things/spin

DUET WITH MYSELF

The function of memory
    My name is Jack
is to soften the blow of death
    I was born
to create the illusion of a self
    far away
though it is also memory
    on the east coast
that creates
    of america
the fear of death
    in a city near the roaring sea

This is the function
    I live
of memory:
    now
to soften
    in the far, far west
the blow of death
    near
to create
    the roaring
the illusion
    of another
of self
    sea

THE SANTA
CROWS IN
SANTA CRUZ

THE SANTA CROWS IN SANTA CRUZ:
A PANTOUM / MOON MADNESS

Where are the Santa Crows?
    Tonight the moon is closest to the earth.
How high do they fly?
    Tonight we will be moon-mad, lunatic
Will they fly down a chiminey?
    How did the moon begin, from chance events
Will they tell you a lie?
    Long ages ago, no one alive from that time.

How high do they fly
    Our "moon light" merely reflection of the sun
When they decide to wing it?
    Do you see the ridges, the things that make it seem
Did she tell me a lie,
    There is a man-face in the middle of the moon,
My mother, when she gave me advice?
    Which, if we stick to facts, is entirely barren
When they decide to wing it,
    No life is there in that brilliant, shining space
You have to put a stop to them.
    "The second brightest celestial body in Earth's sky"
My mother, when she gave me advice,
    And yet we people it with myth, with fables, stories
Usually had no conception of what I really needed
    Reflecting nothing but our deep uncertainty

You have to put a stop to them,
    Of what is real. And now it's Christmas time
The lies people tell you
    The Magi always seem to come at night
Usually with no conception of what you really need,
    The scene is bathed in moonlight—as if that space
No more than the policeman on the corner
    Were reserved for just this dream: a dream of deity

Lies people tell you
    Descending to the earth to save mankind.
They're all right if you can see through them but . . .
    Religions are the harbingers of death
No more is the policeman on the corner
    They tell you that you'll live forevermore
He's chasing dope dealers in the suburbs
    Though what you see around you always dies.

They're all right if you can see through them but
    "If only you'll obey me you will live"
Où sont les neiges d'antan?
    And yet we die, deluded by our saviors.
Chasing dope dealers in the suburbs,
    We live in story; story lives in lies
I became crazed with the need for companionship
    Denying what is obvious to all.

Où sont les neiges d'antan?
    The snows of yesteryear have disappeared
With the Santa Crows.
    The super moon is climbing in the sky
I became crazed with the need for companionship
    Our lives are lunatic: and so we live
Jesus I need to fly down your chiminey!
    And so we die: our longing like the snow.

TURNING 73 (2013)

Today my seventy-fourth year
dawns, in the sweetness of this
California
paradise I came to
fifty years ago.

My heart climbs,
into the wind and the vast
redwoods
and the dreaming, disorderly
cities
with their smells and
violence.
Evil of greed and anger
uncertainty of response
and the death of spirit.

Whatever god nourishes me
has given me a life
of language and music
so that Love may inhabit
the ecstatic evidence
of a consciousness.
that nightly
  presses your body
   against mine.

SPANKING

When I was a child
My mother spanked me
(Are terrorists spanked?
Is spanking terrorism?)
I did not always know
The reason for the spanking
(Are terrorists spanked?
Is spanking terrorism?)
My mother's anger was huge,
Often unpredictable.
And there were terrifying
Threats as well:
Wait till your father gets home
Sometimes said early in the day
So, terrified, I had to wait
For a very long time.
(Are terrorists spanked?
Is spanking terrorism?)
I understood
There were two mommies:
One of them loved me
And gave me kisses,
One of them hated me
And furiously spanked me
Hoping to bend me
To whatever it was that was
Her will.
Once,
When I was too old for the ritual,
I took the stick out of her hands
And broke it in half in front of her.
I can't tell you the pleasure
That action gave me.
She never tried to spank me again.

Spanking is the attempt of power
To assert its will
On the thing it has power over.
My mother never
Changed my behavior:
She simply terrified me.
Are terrorists spanked?
Is spanking a form of terrorism?

JUNE

June 6, 1955

I appeared on *The Ed Sullivan Show* (then called *Toast of the Town*). I was singing with The Port Chester Senior High School Choir. Sullivan was from my hometown, Port Chester N.Y. Apparently he lived there, though I never saw him. We sang "Beyond the Blue Horizon" and "You'll Never Walk Alone." While we sang, "You'll Never Walk Alone, we began, communally, to veer off pitch. A soprano saved us. I don't remember her from school—she was older than I—but she's there on the video, singing. I was very near to Sullivan, in the first row, when he came out to congratulate us. Pearl Bailey was on the show, as was Bob Hope. Hope was the only one who spoke to us. Smith and Dale were also on the bill. They had begun their act in 1902 and were star performers in the years when my father performed. They seemed to be arguing a lot backstage. They must have performed their "Dr. Kronkheit" sketch thousands of times, always successfully. "Are you a doctor?" "I'm a doctor." "I'm dubious." "Glad to know you, Mr. Dubious."

June 5, 2010

Jack Foley Day in Berkeley. I received a Lifetime Achievement Award from The Berkeley Poetry Festival (thank you, Louis Cuneo). Adelle and I performed. We had T shirts manufactured, which we sold. We ended with these speculations, which I had written as a kind of summary. They seem a little glib to me now. The closing passage quotes Baudelaire:

what was the purpose, if purpose there was
why all this fury?
did you hope to change the perceptions
of people at large?
—yes, foolishly.

did you believe that anything you said could affect the immense misconception people call reality? quelle erreur!

—yes, it was a mistake.

so what did it *do*? did you teach anyone anything?

—no.

were you able to change the nature of poetry, even in the smallest way?

—no.

so what reveals itself, admirable author, at this difficult point of your being?

—nothing! j'aime les nuages, les nuages qui passent. I love the passing / clouds. as for poetry, ça m'a donné quelque chose à faire—*it gave me something to do.*

. . .

There are photographs, even video, connected with these events.

June 4, 2016; June 27, 2016

Sad events in June as well. Adelle receiving the news of her cancer (June 4, 2016). Adelle's death (June 27, 2016).

I am a June Bug
I crawl into the month
And receive joy and sorrow
What are days
To a bug?

LOW BLOOD SUGAR INCIDENT

Why did you come?
You called out for me.
What was I doing?
You were standing there. You were confused.
How did I get on the floor?
You sat down.
And then I couldn't get up?
That's right. I tried to bring a chair.
You gave me candy—Life Savers.
That's right. Then you felt better.
I was able to stand up.
Yes.
I don't remember. I must have got up to go to the bathroom.
Yes.

. . .

I went to the bathroom again and then back to bed.
When I closed my eyes I saw small red stars flashing against a black sky.

THE HOSPITAL

Escape with me from the hospital
Into the wild deep sunset outside the window
Into the world of fire
Going down into dark as everything fades
Escape with me from the prison
Which is the hospital
Which is the world
In which I found myself without asking.
Beyond the window.
I am an orphan
Whose father is fire
Whose mother is darkness.
I am the elsewhere
That rings in your ears at the dead end of day
The hospital ends at the window
Escape with me: fly

ELEGY: ROY LISKER

Busker—math whiz—poet—musician—unrelenting gadfly—
How much poorer the world is without you
You made your mark on nothing
Except for the minds that encountered you
And often fed you,
Poverty your bedfellow
Dear man,
Did the Almighty
In whom you did NOT believe
Want someone a little "different" to entertain him?
Berkeley—your violin—*Ferment*—Connecticut—
These years
Let's put them all together in a movie
And run them backwards
Till we reach that blackness
That unknowable stuff
At the beginning
And say that moving into it
Is nothing more
Than entering a dark room
And moving into it
Until you find the light

FATHER'S DAY FOR MY FATHER (1895-1967)

Irish,
slightly taller than I,
thin,
broad forehead,
jet-black hair
with a touch of the dandy
dancer
liked to sing
drank

Irish,

        "We were fairmers"—farmers

slightly taller than I,

        Brother Wayne taught him tap

thin,

        Danced with George "Honeyboy" Evans' Minstrels

broad forehead,

        Sister "Goldie"

jet-black hair

        A Ziegfeld girl

with a touch of the dandy

        "Everybody thought we were sweethearts"

dancer

        "But we weren't"

liked to sing

        Stopped the show once with Irving Berlin's "All By Myself"

drank

        Said, "It must have been the song"

Irish,

        Married my mother on Valentine's Day

slightly taller than I,

        Gave up show business when vaudeville died

thin,

        Took up telegraphy because

broad forehead,

        "It sounded like tap dancing"

jet-black hair

        Watched as my mother grew

with a touch of the dandy

        Increasingly neurotic

dancer

        Had, though Catholic, a previous marriage I knew nothing of

liked to sing

        Until after my mother's death

drank

        Would a drop take on his way home but denied it to my mother

Irish,

Would "disappear" when my mother grew too much for him

slightly taller than I,

She stole things from stores

thin,

He managed a Western Union office

broad forehead,

Felt he was a proper man of the town

jet-black hair

Was embarrassed when my mother

with a touch of the dandy

Was caught red handed, then let off because of his "position" in
      the town

dancer

My mother threatened

liked to sing

To "put her foot

drank

Through the television set"

Irish,

Was generally kind to me

slightly taller than I,

Taught me to tap dance

thin,

Liked the children of the neighborhood

broad forehead,

Who liked him too

jet-black hair

One found him unconscious on the stairs

with a touch of the dandy

"Mommy, Jack's sleeping on the stairs"

dancer

Died before I could wish him goodbye

liked to sing

Held his arms out to me lovingly

drank

Once when I stepped off the train

Irish,

Could be angry, more when I was an adolescent

slightly taller than I,

Didn't think I could go to college

thin,

Feared that I thought myself

broad forehead,

Smarter than he

jet-black hair

                    One day we cleared that up
with a touch of the dandy
                    Gave me a fine childhood
dancer
                    I remember Christmas particularly.
liked to sing
                    Ate all the popcorn
drank
                    In which Adelle and I wrapped a gift we sent him

Irish,
                    Tears, tears for the dear man he was.
slightly taller than I,
                    For the man who could not visit his brother as his brother lay
            dying.
thin,
                    Tears, tears for the lovely stories he told.
broad forehead,
                    For the man who survived World War I, though his brother died
            as a result of the war.
jet-black hair
                    Tears, tears.
with a touch of the dandy
                    Many tears for the good and the bad, the sweet and the violent.
dancer
                    Tears, tears for the songs he sang.
liked to sing
                    For the man who knew famous people, but only Irish ones.
drank
                    Tears for all daddies, tears.

. . .

IN JOYCESPEAK

And so it's Fathers' Day
And the salivation
Of the mighty projanitor
What a middledemaff made we
What a macaroon
For he and the mutt
Gave us the giftie of t-t-tonguetalk
And we him love for the gift and so hymn him.
Gladiflass, daddy, in pieces thou rest.
Morphfilibus from your cadkid: Mich.

THE GLOAMING / MEÁCHAN RUDAÍ

the weight of things
the gloaming

the weight of things
the gloaming

the weight of memory
the weight of the soul

the weight of your terror
and of your refusal

the weight of teeth
the weight of resilience

the weight of narcissism
the weight of your eyes

the fury

        In the world
        No fire
        Is tamed or ready to serve
        Burning
        Is
        Vanishing
        No song
        Burns properly
        In the mind
        In the memory
        Nothing in any fireplace
        But springs forth
        Into the room
        As smoke or heat
        To cause damage
        No cigarette burns
        Properly
        No pipe can be smoked
        So as to confer advantage
        Though hearts burn
        None burn
        Properly
        All cause pain
        Vanishing
        All danger lies here
        Even in the stove

That cooks
The broth
The match
That lights
The dark:
The fever
In this is burning
Burning

BLURB

Although the sonnet may not be the most fashionable of forms in these dark days, there are the wondrous ones of Robert Frost and others who have entered its deep maze. This sonnetarium of my friend Lew is one example of the living form, and there are others. At times I wonder who said sonnets were fit vittles for a worm. With this key Turco unlocks his heart, engaging readers with these witty, passionate, unerring samples of a poet's art. The sonnet!—Is there any cash in it? Its branches grow and grow and are dendritic. Just touch these suns. Scorn not the sonnet, Critic.

SOUTHERN SUITE

"You've had a tornado. Now you'll have us."

THANKSGIVING 2017

Thanks to the companions who make the meal
Special, unlike any other, and the wonderful food
Old memories mingle with present joy
Love lives here in this house
Where the dearest of friends and one
Dearer than any other
Take nourishment together
The delicious food, the splendid light
That gathers around us, young, old
Smiling in autumnal Tennessee
Where the trees are at their most beautiful this time of year—
Sends waves of warmth into the cold air
Where dead leaves fall onto living grass.

ALABAMA AUTUMN

Even new things here
Appear to be old.
History as prevalent as the leaves
This time of year.
Dear friends
Speak of religion
"Are you a Christian?"
"I don't like
What the churches have done to it"
Another about the despicable
Klan
Its murders and violence.
This is the South
Deep, rich and
Murderous in its traditions.
Ice cream store
Since 1918
Klansmen scallywags African Americans
Have eaten here.
Today the Big Game.
The Crimson Tide
Goes down to defeat
Like the old Confederacy
"Mah team lost,"
Said my photographer friend!
"Declension," said John Crowe Ransom,
An elegant Latinate word
To describe the incessant
Sense of loss, crime, courtesy,
The guilt, the "history,"
The looking back.
Deep regret and pride
Are everywhere in the leafy landscape
In which I order
An old-fashioned ice cream soda
And compliment the waitress
On her marvelous chicken soup.

POETS

JAKE: I still don't understand everything about my new Prius.
JACK: But you have a manual.
JAKE: Yes, that's my other car.

TRAVELER'S CREDO: A DUET

Should the sun	*Should the sun*
Rise in the West	*Rise in the West*
Should the dark	*Should the dark*
Resist the light	*Resist the light*
Should the tale	*Should the tale*
Out-tell the teller	*Out-tell the teller*
Should love be known	*Should love be known*
Only among the sequestered few	*Only among the sequestered few*
Should nuns squeal	*Should nuns squeal*
With priests in ecstasy of climax	*With priests in ecstasy of climax*
So should I	*So should I*
On the deep road to Endtown	*On the deep road to Endtown*
Sing my whole heart's	*Sing my whole heart's*
Truth	*Truth*
(Truth!)	*(Truth!)*

THE TRAVELER
In Ye Ole General Store, Florence, Alabama

THE TRAVELERS

This is Bonnie
Of Bonnie & Clyde
In Ye Ole General Store
In Florence, Alabama
Only they are calling themselves
Land & Foley
These days.
Desperados
Terrorizing the South.
No machine guns
Only poetry & visiting
To strike fear
Into the good people
And some relatives
Of Tennessee
And Alabama.

[JAKE BERRY:

They swept through here and terrified the populace all weekend with an assault of poetry, philosophy, music and general goodwill. They completely undermined the general malaise. It will be months before we recover. By then they'll probably return. God help us! I hope they do!]

FAMILY

There's a son talking
  There's a son talking
And a father smiling
  And a father smiling
There's a father talking
  There's a father talking
And a son listening
  And a son listening
There's a woman looking
  There's a woman looking
Red hair gleaming in the light
  Red hair gleaming in the light
And another
  And another
Fixing food—
  Fixing food—
And a father
  And a father
Proud of his son
  Proud of his son
And a son
  And a son

Happy to be with his
Happy to be with his
Father
Father
And the woman
And the woman
Watching them
Watching them
Is happy too
Is happy too
To watch
To watch
And listen
And listen
And speak
And speak
When she wishes.
When she wishes.
Love
Love
Is everywhere
Is everywhere
In this picture
In this picture
In the talk
In the talk
In the food
In the food
In the father's lined
In the father's lined
Hand
Hand
In the son's
In the son's
Intense
Intense
Gesture
Gesture
In the women
In the women
Loved
Loved
By the son
By the son
And by the father.
And by the father.

W.C. HANDY

There, the music
The man with the
Fabulous horn
W.C. Handy
Sharing with
Jelly Roll Morton
The Fatherhood

Of Jazz
His statue
In Florence, Alabama
In deep November.
The music there—
They say it comes
From the Tennessee River
The mud
Of the "Singing River"
To which Tom Hendrix's
Great-Great-Grandmother
Returned
Like a ghost
To which I return
Like a ghost
Each autumn
The music like the leaves
At which Sangye and I
Marveled
Notes like leaves
Everywhere
My shadow in the photo
Hands raised to the camera
The man lurking
In the distance
Photographing me
As I stood
Marveling
At the music
I heard
And did not hear
Handy, the old, blind man
On the Sullivan show
From my childhood
Far from here
And the music I heard
Then and now
Ghost notes
Piercing
The skin of Ego
As I stood with my new love
In the marvelous Alabama air
Which she and I
Breathed, in chorus, together.

FOR THE PAINTER, RICH CURTIS

I dreamed I was in a Rich Curtis painting
One in which the colors come from the soil of the place
That old Georgia shack for instance
Or those reeds by the river
Dreamed I was dreaming in the painting
Thinking I could be the shack or the reeds
As I lay there wondering how
To transcend the skin I was born in
Thinking how I could be a shack or a clump of reeds
Just as the soil of that place
Became a painting became a dream
In the dreaming mind
Of that fabulous man Rich Curtis.

FEMINA

who is the woman behind the woman
the type behind the type
the goddess in the blood—
does she awaken to language?
what makes for the sudden inexplicable connection
that one rather than another?
eyes hair manner intellect
touch?
can we determine "the feminine"?
can we say *why*
the shadow figure within me
wakens in delight
to see your form
to hear your laughter
and whispers
she

I CAN SAY

that I have fallen in love with this autumnal paradise but I cannot say why anymore than I can say why I have fallen in love with a person. So many things connect. I am willing to believe that I lived here once, though so much here is new to me. Is it the landscape, beautiful at this time of year, the dear friends, my son and daughter in law? Is it the air itself? Is it the music that one hears, rising, said Tom Hendrix, from the very river that nourishes this place? Is it the fact that one of my first great literary loves, Thomas Wolfe's *Look Homeward, Angel*, was written by a Southerner? I can't imagine that book coming from anywhere else! There is a deep music here that tears at my heart. I can hear it in Jake Berry's words and songs, see it in Wayne Sides' amazing photographs and in the paintings of Rich Curtis, the latter often incorporating the actual soil of Alabama or wherever he is painting. And there are the films and visions of Chris Mansel. I am a displaced Easterner Westerner longing to become a Southerner, though I live in Northern California, and so I am a Northerner, too. These are the places of the heart.

TENNESSEE, 2018

I have to tell you of my rather amazing adventure with ER on Thanksgiving Night. I usually snack during the day but I didn't on Thanksgiving because I didn't want to spoil my dinner. Had dinner been nearer to the announced time, I think there would have been no problem, but there was a delay and I had a slight low blood sugar incident. I ate something, and the problem seemed to have been solved. Dinner was a delight. I thought the turkey feast would take care of the blood sugar problem and took my regular sugar-diminishing medications. This, it turned out, was a mistake. In the middle of the night, I had ANOTHER low blood sugar incident, this one much more intense than the other one. I have no recollection of exactly what happened or what I said (Sangye told me I slurred my speech) but it terrified Sangye, especially since, for whatever reason, I kept indicating my left arm. Sangye was afraid I was having a heart attack! Had she given me some candy, I think I would have immediately come out of the attack, but I was in some sort of alternate space, a kind of live dream, and couldn't tell her to do that. She called the night clerk who definitely agreed that I was acting strangely. I had fallen about a year earlier, and someone asked me whether I was all right mentally. To show that I was, I recited the opening lines of *Paradise Lost*. It worked fine then, so I tried it again. This time—given my altered state—it didn't work so well. Neither Sangye nor the night clerk had any idea of what I was trying to accomplish by my recitation. So she phoned 911. At about 5:30 a.m. in come these rather burly gentlemen. They put me on a gurney and then in an ambulance and off we went to the hospital. On the way they squirted sugar water into my mouth—the equivalent of candy!—so by the time I reached the hospital I was pretty much recovered though a bit chilly in my jammies. The hospital staff and the doctor were very nice. The doctor looked me up on *Wikipedia* and showed some interest in reading something I'd written. Since at that point I was fine and there were no complicating issues, I told Sangye not to alarm Sean and Kerry with what had happened. Throughout all this, Sangye was very sweet, loving, efficient, and a little scared. The hospital staff gave me a warm blanket—it was COLD out—and we took LYFT back to the hotel. The doctor suggested that I shouldn't drive to Florence on Friday, but I told him I'd be fine, which I was. We munched on candy along the way.

In California, every night, the DDD Monster is tucked into bed by a figure he calls "The Angel." "Looks a lot like Sangye," he says. ("It IS Sangye," says The Angel.) He loves being tucked into The Angel's wings—which look a lot like a warm blanket. When we returned to the hotel in Tennessee, The Angel once again appeared and tucked the Monster in. "Looks a lot like Sangye," he muttered as he happily fell asleep.

THANKSGIVING NIGHT, 2017

Here I am in the Tennessee night
listening for the sounds of Tennessee
What tenderness accosts me
What power of remembering

Seeing
the trees of Tennessee
the leaves that have not fallen
in their tenacious clinging.

I would nest among

these brittle tender leaves
these roaring sights
these things
of Tennessee

. . .

IN IMITATION OF XU ZHIMO

Leaving Tennessee
on a gray cold morning
work done here
accents singing—
disturbing nothing
leaving as quietly

as a leaf

falls

SHILLELAGH SONGS

SHILLELAGH SONGS

I never owned
I never owned
a shillelagh these songs
a shillelagh these songs
are all
are all
though the thing
though the thing
is a weapon
is a weapon
a cane (useful in my old
a cane (useful in my old
age) a symbol
age) a symbol
of a place I never
of a place I never
visited except in
visited except in
imagination
imagination
The dark
The dark
Irishman
Irishman
of my imagination
of my imagination
perhaps carries one:
perhaps carries one:
he will not use it
he will not use it
for violence
for violence

SANGYE

Can you say she took your breath away
Yes, I can say that
But you talked on to her
    And that
        Required
            Breath
Can you say
She was beautiful
Yes, I can say that
    Her hair especially was beautiful
        And her serious
            Eyes
    But she was also
        Exceptionally kind
She listened when you spoke
    Yes, and laughed
        When I said
            Something amusing
Yet her laughter seemed almost
    Reluctant
        As if she couldn't quite help herself
As if something came from within
(As something came from within me)

There was no way on earth we could be lovers

As I left she said, "It was wonderful to meet you"
I thanked her for being so considerate

        Her hair moved often
           As she moved

12/28/16

"Who says we're incompatible?
You're Buddhism
I'm Vaudeville"

*

"It's karma, baby"

*

I made a remark
About how sometimes
Unconventional solutions
Work very well for me.
You said
(Looking at me with those deep, penetrating lamps of yours),
"Like me."

LUNA PLENA

O mOOn
O luna
plena
O bright
I
in the sky
O full
O fOOl's
mOOn
O
luna
O
Beauty
O
pleine
O
clair
de lune
i mOan
in your light,
rOund
O
for Sangye

GATE, GATE, PARAGATE, PARASAMGATE, BODHI SVAHAA!

Going, going, going on beyond
Always going on beyond,
Always becoming Buddha
Going, going,
Going on beyond,
Beyond this beyond
The
Always going on beyond
Always becoming
Buddha
In the dark of our lives
This song
Awakens life
Awakens me to longing
A longing song that rises
In the heart of the morning in the sudden flush of love for Sangye
As I see the Buddha (Sangye)
Not as a person but as a possibility
As the never ending
Always beginning
Always going on
Beyond
Arising in my heart   in the deep ground
Of being

*

shadows move across my table
old age does not mean
difficulty with thought
(though names may disappear)
old age is to be ravaged
by memory, people alive once,
no longer yet
present in the mind (from this
the notion of ghosts?)
people who can no longer answer
but whose words stay lodged
in the web-filled smoky attic of your
busy consciousness and at times
if they were dear
bring tears
and thoughts of the strangeness of death
that something that was

could cease absolutely
and without recourse
of any kind—no longer "there"
shadows move constantly in the room
against the wall
at this time of day
at this moment
this closed particularity
in the vast river we call
years
years

SANGYE 3/2/17:

Sonnet XVII by Pablo Neruda . . . sent to Jack by Sangye:

I do not love you as if you were salt-rose, or topaz,
or the arrow of carnations the fire shoots off.
I love you as certain dark things are to be loved,
in secret, between the shadow and the soul.
I love you as the plant that never blooms
but carries in itself the light of hidden flowers;
thanks to your love a certain solid fragrance,
risen from the earth, lives darkly in my body.
I love you without knowing how, or when, or from where.
I love you straightforwardly, without problems or pride;
so I love you because I know no other way
than this: where I does not exist, nor you,
so close that your hand on my chest is my hand,
so close that your eyes close as I fall asleep.

—Pablo Neruda, translated by Mark Eisner

JACK'S RESPONSE:

"I do not love you as if you were salt-rose, or topaz,
or the arrow of carnations the fire shoots off"
In the sweet darkness, when we have closed the door
And adjusted the pillows and said the word "dearest"
In the flame that comes to us in that darkness
In the light of the mind and body
We kiss and hold each other, mindful of the bliss
That comes to all animals, to all sentient beings
And wonder at the luck
That stretches itself throughout the room
As we merge
And my body becomes yours
And yours mine,
"so close that your eyes close as I fall asleep"

DEATH / LIFE

Death said to Life, May I have this dance?
Life said, Yes, but don't step on my toes.
Death said, I can't promise that.
The music is jagged, the dance floor uneven.
Everything lives, but everything dies.
May I waltz you around while the life blood flows?
Life said, Yes, and offered her lips
And offered her breasts
And offered her love to the Whirl of Death.

EASTER RAIN,

we hear it as it falls
in its steadiness
under the eaves
upstairs
as we lie
happy in one another's arms—
pain
momentarily vanquished.
soothing patient
    ancient sounds   *(soothing patient*
           ancient sounds)
chants of resurrection
heard by billions
of lovers
and sinners
too

FOR SANGYE-LA

You're sleeping now
Deep into the morning
How brave you were
To speak so frankly
And so sweetly
To the one you loved best in the world
I love it
When your eyes open
And I see the sun.

. . .

You let me see
Your secret places
And they all shine
And make sweet, sweet music.

DUET

play with my hair
play with my hair
night comes near
night comes near
the deep air
the deep air
romantic strains
romantic strains
open my heart
open my heart
bring me near
bring me near
to fear and desire
to fear and desire
prayer has no efficacy
prayer has no efficacy
Light
Light
opens me
opens me
Love
love
bends to the dance
bends to the dance

SANGYE SLEEPS,

The graph of a mind moving
Sangye sleeps
The path of the wind moving
Sangye sleeps
The path of the wind loving
She curls
In the blanket
Like the wind
Inhabiting a tree
Like the mind
Inhabiting a subject
Like a child
In a blanket
Sangye
Is beautiful in the morning
Like a leaf
Appearing on a branch
In the bright / morning
Light:
The path of a mind
      Loving

["This poetry is a picture or graph of the mind moving" (Philip Whalen)]

ONDINE

*"Oh, how difficult it is to live among you, where what
has happened can never again not have happened. How
terrible to live where a word can never be unspoken
and a gesture can never be unmade."*
—*Jean Giraudoux,* Ondine (1938)

Ondine, Ondine,
Your name means "water"
Beautiful
Maiden,
Ondine
"the difference here   *[The men watch her in the tank:*
is that the heroine   *some see a fish;*
is a fish"   *some see a woman;*
silken   *some see a young girl,*
inhabitant of the waves   *(*ondes*) their daughter,*
Highest good is like you,   *even the childless ones.]*
Ondine
Mercurial,
"Changefull
Potency"
Sweet,
Feeling creature
Soulless
But full of heart
And deep compassion
What will the human world
Do with you
What will the knight you love
Cause you to feel
Ondine, Ondine
As you move
In your water world
("She swims
Occasionally")
Wave
Upon
Wave

(Nous sommes sur les ondes)	*(We are on the waves)*
Princesse	*Princess*
Du Monde	*Of the*
Alluvial,	*Alluvial*
Du Monde	*World,*
Fictive et	*Of the fictional*
Non	*Non fictional*
Fictive:	*World:*
Tes yeux	*Your eyes*
Tes yeux—	*Your eyes—*
Ton sourire—	*Your smile—*
Tes nageoires—	*Your fins—*
Ondine	*Ondine*

BIRTHDAY POEM FOR SANGYE (2018)

There is a long lake
And trees surrounding it
In a womb-like formation
With marvelous, shifting
Clouds in the deep blue sky.
I know this lake
Doesn't exist
But I think of it
As where you were born
In Oregon
A womb place
To which your mind returns
And to which, now,
My mind has access.
I think of you
Emerging from it
With the magical name
Sangye
Defining you.
There are birds
In this forest
But they are silent
As your consciousness
Arises
And comes into the world.
None of this is real.
It is story
Something I made up
To fill my mind
With what I cannot
Know:
Your origin.
Were there wings
That you discarded
At the lake
And a quiet, bearded boatman
To deliver you to this world?
Was there another you
Before this one?
What was your history?
What was the little girl
Who looked around her
At a world
Which at times

Would be cruel to her?
What lies were you told?
What truths?
What is it that makes you
Sometimes shudder?
Is it the memory
Of that lake, that forest
Those marvelous,
Abandoned
Wings?
Did the boatman betray you?
None of this is true
And yet truth enters into it
And a magic world
That radiates
Delight and fear and love.
What were they, those clouds,
Those trees, that lake, those wings diaphanous?
Could they protect
The living soul
That arose in magic
And carried with it
Traces
Of that Nowhere,
That magic Land
Through all your loved, tumultuous, passionate, fiery days.

SANGYE GIVES ME A CD

she is looking for the love
  she is looking for the love
she hears in the songs
  she hears in the songs
she is looking for a song
  she is looking for a song
of love
  of love
she is looking
  she is looking
in the words and
  in the words and
sounds
  sounds
for a music
  for a music
to which the words and
  to which the words and
sounds refer
  sounds refer
she is looking
  she is looking
in words and sounds
  in words and sounds
she is
  she is
listening
  listening

MONTHLY

the blood flow comes
    It's my period again
and turns your body
    I've been spotting
into a passageway
    We need to buy
for a river
    Some more
that will neither
    Tampax
be denied
    Look:
nor quite contained:
    I've bled through
the blood flow
    My skirt,
reminds
    My panties.
that we are makers
    I wish it would come
but also that
    At a more convenient
we die
    Time.
even as we make

HIS WORDS

"the minute I saw you it was darkness
depths in your eyes depths in your mouth
there were no heights no skies
only the rushing tide of the deep
taking me away with you"
—lines by Argüelles
carry me into myself
conjure meeting Sangye
the sudden extraordinary interest
the beauty of her eyes
her speech
all I remember
the sudden hope (which seemed insane)—
words dig
into shards of time
inhabit them
Sangye and I, the room, the people,
David's dying—
all of that in the words of my dear friend Argüelles
who experienced none of it
but whose words are an open door
through which I pass
visible, invisible, strange, violently alive.

ANNIVERSARY (2019)

My mind returns continually to our first meeting
That day when we first spoke:
In the midst of what should have been
A sorrowful occasion—a dear friend dying—
Suddenly life interrupted everything
And shouted at me in all its dearness: *she*
I don't think it's possible to forget such a moment
Even in old age, when men "forget things"
And now the turning of two years
Since that "first date": what are you doing on Valentine's Day
Innocently asked but responded to
With desire I had not felt since who knows when
You were coordinating the visitors to your stepfather
So you had to move away but you kept returning
And now, after two years,
After two years,
Desire remains and increases and burns
In this strange, amazing, lustful, loving old age.

FOR SANGYE ON VALENTINE'S DAY, 2018

La Sangye d'un Poète
moves around the house like a vivid shadow
wearing red, wearing green, wearing blue
colors of light, as she moves
wearing a shine that catches me
and speaks, a vivid, beautiful shadow,
sends notes, smiles, comments,
agrees, disagrees, tells me I'm handsome
that I look good in blue
(O flattery that I may believe!)
asks me to rub salve on her back
to relieve the pain she sometimes
feels as she moves as she lives
and listens, in my gaze and out of it,
a shade more vivid than the furniture
that watches her and beckons
I think of *Paramasiva*
when he opens his eyes the world manifests
when he closes them the world retracts
to its latent state within him
he makes the impossible
possible
as does she
as she moves as she talks
in this deep, wild house
of Shiva

SANGYE AT TASHI CHOLING

Lady,
with your face in the light,
Lady of light,
blessed by the sun,
prayer flag whirling before you
blue of deep night
you stand smiling
as colors gather around you
Sangye
at a height of love
Sangye
dreaming of benefit
to all sentient beings

WILD GINGER:
a new year's poem (2019)

Anniversary =
The turning of a year
Anni, of a year, -versary, turning
The same word for poetry: "verse": a turning
Re-verse: turning again, turning back
Janus
The god who faces in both directions
The pinpoint on which we stand
Anniversary
The flight from, towards
I am calling this poem
Wild Ginger
Though I don't know why
Except that I love
Both ginger and wildness
And perhaps because today's sky
Makes me feel
The thrill of possibility
A turning
(The lights on the tree
Remind us—my love and me—of things long past)
I gave a child
A toy dog
And turned again
Towards childhood
Hers and mine
Anniversary
The turn of a year
The turn of a child's head
In laughter
The turn of my mind
Towards the future
And
The past
(The lights on the tree
Remind us—my love and me—of things long gone and passt)

CHANSON D'AMOUR ET DE LA LITÉRATURE

J'ai
Tous les livres du monde
Et tous les livres
Disent que je t'aime
Vraiment?
Bien sur.
Les livres Scandinaves?
Oui, même les livres Scandinaves
Les livres d'Allemagne?
Oui, les livres d'Allemagne
Les livres du Sahara?
Oui, oui, même ces livres
Tous les livres du monde
Disent
"Je t'aime"

. . .

C'est pour Sangye, ce poème?
Bien sur!

SHE IS IN MY LIFE!

innocence
   innocence
matched with
   matched with
intelligence
   intelligence
sweetness
   sweetness
matched with
   matched with
guile
   guile
(& wit)
   (& wit)
a deep
   a deep
awareness of
   awareness of
suffering
   suffering
("I have been in pain most of my life")
   ("in pain most of my life")
desire
   desire
matched with
   matched with
compassion
   compassion
fear
   fear
of
   of
abandonment
   abandonment
fear
   fear
of
   of
sleep
   sleep
wish
   wish
for structure
   for structure

&
    &
cleanliness
    cleanliness
shy
    shy
but with extraordinary
    but with extraordinary
capacity for listening
    capacity for listening
wish
    wish
for the holiness
    for the holiness
of Buddhahood
    of Buddhahood
incredibly
    incredibly
passionate
    passionate
eyes
    eyes

LIGHT

FOR WILLIAM BLAKE'S BIRTHDAY (NOV. 28)

". . . nunnes blake" (Geoffrey Chaucer/John Skelton)

Today's the day of William Blake
Who was also "William Black"
Listen to the little boy
Singing of his bitter lack:

My soul is white, sang William Black
The English boy is white as snow
But I'm the furious jungle beast
Who feasts on everything below

I'm William Black sang William Blake
I am a riddle to your soul
Shall I the Christian God forsake
To make a new bright-shining foal?

For William Black *is* William Blake
I make the fur, the flesh, the shell
I made the Songs of Innocence
And of Experience I tell

I sing of joy I sing of woe
I sing the Everlasting Night
I sing the little jungle boy
Whose soul is dark, bereaved of Light

I'm William Black sang William Blake
I have a warring in my soul
I shall the Christian God forsake
To make a new, bright-shining foal.

FOR KAITLIN & HANNAH,
DEAR CHILD FRIENDS

Kaitlin & Hannah
Hannah & Kaitlin
Had an adventure
In a town called Childhood

Hannah saw a bird
And Kaitlin saw a bird
But the bird said Au contraire
I'm not a bird I'm really a free verse poet

A free verse poet
Said Kaitlin
I've never heard of such of thing
Nonetheless, said the bird,
That's what I am

Hannah said, Will you favor us
With one of your verses
Certainly, said the bird
CHIRP CHIRP CHIRP CHIRP CHIRP CHIRP CHIRP
Pretty good, hah?

Well, said Kaitlin,
I would like it better if I understood it
It's poetry
Said the bird
You're not supposed to understand it

Hmmmm, said Hannah
I don't think you're
A very good
Free verse poet

Neither do I, said Kaitlin

You're right, said the bird
It isn't free verse at all:
I charge:
Fifteen cents, please.

Hmph, said Hannah
And Hmph, said Kaitlin
And they didn't give him any money
But went home
And wrote a free verse poem

That rhymed.

THE MARX BROTHERS MEET DONALD TRUMP

CHICO: Hey, whatsa you name?

GROUCHO: Rufus T. Trump

CHICO: What kinda name is that?

GROUCHO: Why that's a very good name. That's an American name.

CHICO: I'm-a name-a Chico. Atsa American name too.

GROUCHO: Chico doesn't sound so American to me. It sounds . . . uh . . . Mexican.

CHICO: Mexican? Nah. I'm-a from the Bronx.

GROUCHO: Mexican, eh. Are you sure you're not an illegal immigrant.

CHICO: I'm-a don't know. My parents they never mentioned it. They were too busy crossing the border into Brooklyn.

GROUCHO: Well, it's something your parents should have discussed with you.

CHICO: Hey, where are you from?

GROUCHO: I'm from Queens, NY.

CHICO: Queens! We no got a queen in America. That sounds-a pretty foreign to me. Maybe *you* are a immlegal illigrant.

GROUCHO: A immlegal illigrant?

CHICO: Atsa right. I think I better call a cop. Oh, here's-a one now.

HARPO appears.

GROUCHO: This is a cop?

CHICO: Well, he's sort of a cop. He's a airport official. He's a gonna put you on a plane. He's a gonna show you what-a we do with immlegal illigrants.

HARPO laughs silently. He is wearing a policeman's cap.

GROUCHO: Listen. He's got no authority here.

CHICO: Are you-a kiddin'? He wrote a lotta books. He's a great big authority. Show him.

HARPO produces pages and pages and pages. He tosses them into the air.

CHICO: What-a you do for a livin'?

GROUCHO: I'm a quizmaster on the television.

CHICO: That's-a what I thought. We no want-a the quiz master. We got rid of the masters and-a the slaves a long while ago. Show him your power.

HARPO produces a huge hammer.

CHICO: That's-a what I call power!

HARPO scowls and threatens GROUCHO with the hammer.

GROUCHO: Hey, he's dangerous.

CHICO: That's-a what I said.

HARPO swings mightily with the hammer. He misses GROUCHO and hits CHICO instead. CHICO falls down.

CHICO arises. Hey, you supposed to hit-a *him*.

HARPO looks sad and begins to cry.

CHICO It's-a ok, it's-a ok. Next time aim a little better.

HARPO begins to swing again.

Hey wait a minute, says GROUCHO. I tell you what. Let's hold an election instead.

CHICO: You wanna hold an election?

Sure, says GROUCHO. I have the votes right here.

GROUCHO reaches into his pocket and pulls out a number of pieces of paper.

GROUCHO: Let's count them.

OK, says CHICO, only I don't-a count so good.

GROUCHO: Let me do it for you.

GROUCHO counts the votes carefully and puts them back in his pocket.

GROUCHO: Just as I thought. I won.

CHICO: I guess-a that's the American way.

GROUCHO: Yes, it is. Fair and square.

CHICO: OK, you the president.

GROUCHO: Yep, that's me. Thanks, fellas.

CHICO: Hit him anyway.

HARPO does.

GROUCHO falls to the ground. HARPO and CHICO drag his body into a near-by plane. The plane has a destination written in large letters across its windshield. It says NOWHERE.

That's-a good, says CHICO. It looks-a like that's-a where we all going.

HARPO begins to cry again.

Suddenly GROUCHO awakens and begins to sing, "Hooray for Captain Spaulding, the African explorer." Let's appoint him to the Supreme Court! HARPO hits GROUCHO again.

The theme song from *You Bet Your Life* fills the air. They all get in the plane. The plane flies off to its destination.

I awake saying, "Hmmmmm, was that a dream?"

O TEMPORA! O MORES!
JOHN ASHBERY

You know, I can't do a thing with my
hair, this is the worst it's been in several
years. With weather like this who can
even make an effort. *Mon dieu.*
Do you know the story of Little
Red Riding Hood? Well, there's this
Little girl and of course she's wearing
A red hood so you can see her a mile off
In the forest and she has this little basket
To bring to grandma and there's this wolf who's
Eaten grandma (not too tasty a dish there)
And Fantômas, where is Fantômas when we really
Need him. For that matter where is
Anybody anyway, really, if you
Get down to it, and that's where we are.
White lilies in the bowl no not the toilet
Bowl the vase over there, you ninny. Don't
Pronounce it "vase" to rhyme with "ace."
Pronounce it "vase" to rhyme
With Gaz in Gaza strip, and speaking of strips
(Get your mind out of the gutter I was going to talk
About the comics) . . . Ho hum it's so boring in this room
With just you to talk to and me sitting here
Blah blah blah I think poetry ought to rhyme don't you
I wrote a sestina once who cares blah blah
Where is Frank O'Hara? Oh yes, I remember
And Bunny, you remember Bunny? All in the same
"Interminable," as the French would say,
And further as the French would say: *merde*
Oh, the fifties, nobody would want *them* back
Nobody wants us back either,
Especially after our behavior at Jeremy's last party
Disgraceful, yes? O tempora, O mores!
I think of *The Yellow Stream*—not the movie
But the novel by
I.P. Daly.
White lilies resemble the stars that frighten us as we sleep.

John Ashbery
Whose work some people understand
While others say they understand it but don't
And others declare it
Incomprehensible—

Has died
And left a hole in American poetry
In the American language
That absolutely no one—not I, not anyone—can fill.

IS IT BACH THAT I HEAR
OR JUST A COLE PORTER SONG?

How to praise Cole Porter
How to respond
To a language
That raises us into another world
"My will is strong but my won't is weak"
How to praise
His ways
And days
Lightness
Is an infinite possibility
In a world of finitude.
This
Is
Tinpantithesis
The mind's capacity
To transcend itself.
How to praise a rich man's democratic impulses
How to know
The deeply conflicted consciousness
That owned millions
But worked on Broadway,
That praised women but wrote the word "gay"
Into a verse about George Raft
"The most paradoxical man ever to invade show business"
How to tell the millions of people who sing his songs
That he was not just another songwriter
But a gift from the heart of American culture
That it was his lifelong depression and its silences
And the pain and loss of a leg that finally took him
Despite his love of swank
So that, after *Aladdin*, he never wrote another song.
"It was sad seeing him so depressed,
Knowing in your heart that he no longer wanted to live."
Haunted by failure, by mother, by the constantly challenging terms of American
   success
And its relationship to his gay, snobbish, brilliant, bon vivant consciousness,
He was ourselves: puzzled, successful in a malodorous, rinky-tink world.
My story is much too sad to be told.
Legless.
"Me. Mighty me."

THE BIRTHDAYS

For james joyce and koon woon

"He may be a great genius, but he certainly has a dirty mind" (Nora Barnacle)

And which of us great geniuses has NOT a dirty mind? Not a lot of them I'd say. Is not dirt where spirit comes from, though it aspires (to breathe upon, to blow upon, to breathe) the mind goes upward, blown away and blown. Felicitous fecundity! And riverrun, past Eve and Adam's, from swerve of shore to bend of bay, brings us by a commodious vicus of recirculation back to Howth Castle and Environs

HERE COMES EVERYBODY

And every body too. And every Bodhi. Isn't it sleep that slips us, isn't it dark that tells of the everlasting all alluvial. So it comes in the night when the tide falls on us and the dayglow vanishes and the dreamtime the false death comes. Father of Otters, the odd ones, the writers and wrongers, the singers and wringers the ringmen the holy the rinpoche the precious the jewel the knife in the mind that kills all the deadlines and reminds and respects the weirdos the well-wishers the wonts and the wants

Two friends of the heart came into the world today came into the scream of consciousness and paddled their way along it to the heart of the bardo. One was an Irishman of the great gifts and the other a Chinese a giftie too and they are otters both of great skull and the skill of the fingers.

May the memory of one and the day of thee other shine with the wonner of wonders and may the terror fall out of the word terrific.

Good birds to them both, and the ghost that flies with (as said by the priestman) ah! bright wings!

DREAM, SOUND, BLUE, LIGHT—WORDS FOUND FREQUENTLY IN AL YOUNG'S WORK

how does one measure
intellect
how does one measure
heart
words are
doors
deeds are
doors
the terms *dream, sound, blue, light*
are a measure
Al Young
is a thinking being
a political animal, *Zôion politikòn*
living in the *polis*, Berkeley
I see him there
measuring flowers
photographing dreams
looking to the blue
sky
standing between the inner & the outer
speaking
sounding
dreaming
shedding light
in the bright Berkeley dawn

STAN &

They are called "The Boys"
Because they are child-like.
In the film, *Stan & Ollie*
Steve Coogan
& John C. Reilly
Play Laurel & Hardy.
Coogan is good
Weaving in & out of Stanie
But Reilly
Transforms the film
Never for a moment
Do we doubt him.
Dialogue
That verges on cliché
And which doubtless
L&H never spoke
Becomes stunningly real
Because of Reilly.
I don't know anything
About ghosts,
I don't know anything
About "channeling,"
But I can say this:
It is an act of utter transcendence
For a man to become
Another
And Reilly, whose middle name is Christopher,
Does this.
He is not the Christ-bearer
But the bearer of the spirit
Of a dead comedian.
There are no false moments.
There is no dead air.
There is no confusion.
Je est autre.

WORSHIPPING AS A CATHOLIC

NO ONE
at Our Lady of Mercy Church in Port Chester
thought like a hippy

*

trying to figure out
from my Sunday Missal
where in the Latin
the priest was

*

caught between
two women
with conflicting
perfumes

*

(close the little door)
bless me, father,
for I have sinned.
with yourself
or with others, my son?

*

Jack,
have you ever considered
becoming a priest?

*

no, Jack, I have never read
Dante's
Divine Comedy

*

Catholicism
might be considered
one of the great historical triumphs
of Homoeroticism
and
Lesbianism,
he suggested
with a leer.

*

if you miss Mass on Sunday
and you die
you will burn in hell

*

mom, why don't you
go to Mass?
I got nothing to wear

*

Holy Father,
is George Bernard Shaw in hell?
he never
went to Mass

*

everyone
stand up
and say hello
to Father

*

kneel
stand up
kneel
stand up
kneel

*

Holy Father,
do Protestants
die
too?

*

my mother on her death bed:
"I'm going down, down"
"No, mom, you're going up, up"
"Not after what I've done,

Not after what I've done."

WITH APOLOGIES TO E.B. WHITE AND "I PAINT WHAT I SEE"

"What do you want when you want a wall?"
Said 'Frisco's Nancy Pelosi
"Do you want to keep out anyone at all
Or is it political folderol?"
"I want a BIG wall," said the Donald.

"And will this big wall compensate at all"
Said 'Frisco's Nancy Pelosi
"For the many times that you trip and fall
For the lies that you constantly tell to all
For the fact you're the worst president of all?"
"I want a BIG wall," said the Donald.

"Well, you're not gonna get your wall at all"
Said Madam Speaker Pelosi
"For asking those billions you've got some gall
Is it because there is something SMALL
That you have to make up for and so you stall—
As a president you get a low C."
"I want a BIG wall," said the Donald

"I want a BIG wall, I want such a wall
As nobody ever has seen at all
To keep all those Mexicans deep in thrall
(Devious drug dealing Mexicans all!)
My father gave me a lot of dough
Why won't Congress keep up the flow
Why is it such a terrible pill
I'm asking only a mere five bil
Dear Nance, how the future will be so rosy
When everyone's White we can be real cozy
And after all,
'Twill be MY wall . . ."
"We'll see if it will," said Pelosi.

> *King Liar sits in a house of White*
> *King Liar visits the land with Blight*
> *Unevenly does this man dispense*
> *And by his side is the foul fool Pence*
>
> *Chaos, says Liar, is what I am*
> *A man of business, my business Sham*
> *I say I'm an ordinary guy like you*
> *But even the dogs know it isn't true*

My orange hair feels the lack of Hope
Sometimes I flatter sometimes I grope
I have a wife and a son in law
Who drinks Russian vodka and flouts the law

The law, c'est moi, says busy Liar
Watch me burn with my pants on fire,
I know for what you fools are yearning
But look, the country is burning. Burning!

GUIT
ARRA

a
wo-
man
by
gram-
mar
sound
hole
sings
ena-
mored
I am
soy guitarrista I
have played this majestic
instrument this wooden cry
since childhood guitarrista
touching the neck touching
the body until sound
emerges chordal or
single notes guitarrista have
lent my inadequate voice to its
wonderful wailings guitarrista at
times at night under the discerning
moon in the silence of darkness list-
ening to the sound earth makes
upon these wondering
wonderful strings

THERE ARE, SAID THELONIOUS MONK,

no wrong notes on the piano
There are, said Charles Ives,
no wrong notes
If you look for compassion
In the violent
Twentieth Century
Look here
Look to music

TWO POEMS, RECITED SEPARATELY, THEN SIMULTANEOUSLY

O to sound like Joseph Spence
O what joy I could dispense
With those owl-ly, growly sounds
In a voice like coffee grounds
His falsetto was a bleat
Like a chicken caught in heat
I play dem all, the roars and dives
He would be beloved of Ives
Come sweet seven, come eleven
You will get a trip to heaven
Who says music must make sense
O to sound like Joseph Spence

Have you ever heard
Lead Belly tap dance?
He could do that too.
He had that big 12-string guitar
And those big hands to play it
He used them once to kill a man
But it doesn't matter the music goes on
In the end, though, he couldn't play
This is a song about a great passionate
Humorous intelligent very well dressed
Black man who had
Genius in his hands

THREE SONG LYRICS

WITHOUT YOU

I wonder what I was
Without you
What anybody does
Without you
I know there was a world
But it was dull and gray
And I was Mister Nowhere
Going on his way

I wonder if I sighed
Without you
I hadn't any pride
Without you
I think there must have been
Some kind of world out there
I can't remember when
I took a breath of air

There must have been some love
Cause love is everywhere
The moon was up above
The sun was somewhere there
I can't remember where

I can't recall my life
Without you
I must have had a life
Without you
I never caught my breath
I never stopped to stare
It wasn't life but death
Without you
    for Sangye

SADO WITH HIM

I got a girl
Who is so refined
She's got a girl friend
But I don't mind

Life is a blur
Not a game or a whim
When you're maso with her
And sado with him

This girl of mine
They say she's bi
Cause she likes a girl
And she likes a guy

Nobody wins
Whatever occurs
When you're sado with him
And maso with her

She treats me mean
But it's love I know
She gets beat down
By her lover-foe

I wish I could find
A cure to engage
Her whirling mind
Goes from cage to cage

Nobody wins
Whatever occurs
When you're sado with him
And maso with her

WILL IT EVER STOP RAINING

Whaddaya think?
Whaddaya know?
Will it ever stop raining?
Will the sun shine again
Will it be as it was
Or is my complaining
Nothing but feigning

Whaddaya think?
Whaddaya know?
Will you come back tomorrow?
Will our love be a fact
Will it be as it was
Will a sweet second act
Put an end to my sorrow?

Life moves along
But not like a song
More like a tidal wave!
We're here and we're there
Who said life was fair
You're right and then suddenly—wrong

Whaddaya think?
Whaddaya know?
Will it end, my complaining?
Is it passing, this storm
That knocks us all down
Is it safe, is it warm
In some other town?
Whaddaya think?
Will it ever
Will it ever
Will it ever stop raining?

for Al Young

115

SPARRING WITH BEATNIK GHOSTS: THE DANCE

for Daniel Yaryan (who coined the admirable phrase)

corso ginsberg kerouac
climb into the ring
they shadow punch me
I feint pretend to throw a punch
jack micheline comes in
lays a good one on my chest
kirby doyle gets his irish up and dances around me
I feel nothing but pretend to react
then william burroughs tries an uppercut
and amazingly kerouac's saintly brother gerard
whose beatific smile makes me drop my guard for a moment
then lucien carr then phil whalen
then lew welch hits me with a wild one to my eyebrow
which I don't feel
and kerouac's mother lays a right cross on me
what fancy footwork as she moves away from my feigned jab
cassady comes in and laughs but can do nothing
ted joans comes in swinging
david meltzer explains what a mikveh is and chuckles
huncke says, "I'm beat"
lamantia hits me with an exquisite corpse
norse and wieners offer a room in their hotels
they are all dead leaves falling
in an autumn without end
luanne henderson sticks her tongue out at me
elise cowen commits suicide in front of me (again)
joan burroughs pretends to shoot me with her fingers "bang bang"
philomene long offers me flowers and a guitar
and lands one on my epidermis
I punch at them and hit nothing but air
their punches land but do me no harm
it is not a prizefight but a dance
it is not a dance but a whirling dream
in which we all laugh as we spar
yr all BEATNIKS! says mrs gechtoff
yr all BEATNIKS! says mrs gechtoff
and stuart perkoff says what's a beatnik
no one answers but the dance, the dance goes on

FACEBOOK (FEB. 1): "IT'S JACK FOLEY'S BIRTHDAY"

It's Jack Foley's birthday
But it isn't mine
Jack Foley came into the world today
But Jack Foley isn't me
Yet I am Jack and Foley too
So perhaps it's my birthday after all
No man (nor woman)
Knows his birth
But for the words of others
It's Langston Hughes' birthday
And the day reserved
For the Irish Bridget
And the beginning of Black History Month
So who wouldn't be proud to be born this day!
I'm proud to be born
On Jack Foley's birthday
Though I'm Jack Foley
And I wasn't.

RANT, AFTER FLORIDA

How do we mourn for children
How do we mourn for children
How do we mourn for these defenseless ones
How do we mourn for these defenseless ones
How do we cry out against
How do we cry out against
A future cut off at the root
A future cut off at the root
We call it senseless and look for reasons
We call it senseless and look for reasons
Blame the victims blame the authorities
Blame the victims blame the authorities
Blame everything except the true cause
Blame everything except the true cause
Which lies all around you as plain as day
Which lies all around you as plain as day
In every television show in every news story
In every television show in every news story
In every comic book in every political statement
In every comic book in every political statement
In every action hero in every piece
In every action hero in every piece
Of parental guidance in every song in rap
Of parental guidance in every song in rap
Hip hop pop old movies all university syllabi books
Hip hop pop old movies all university syllabi books
Talk shows in every assassination and
Talk shows in every assassination and
Every assassination attempt in the National
Every assassination attempt in the National
Rifle Association in any political party left
Rifle Association in any political party left
Right or center in every attempt to better the situation
Right or center in every attempt to better the situation
In capitalism in socialism in radical in conservative
In capitalism in socialism in radical in conservative
In the banks in auto dealerships in my mother's
In the banks in auto dealerships in my mother's
Complaints about my behavior in prisons in freedom
Complaints about my behavior in prisons in freedom
In the latest movie about love in Christianity in Judaism in Islam in Buddhism in the
In the latest movie about love in Christianity in Judaism in Islam in Buddhism in the
KKK in the Young Men's Christian
KKK in the Young Men's Christian

Association in the collision of all these things
Association in the collision of all these things
In the consciousness of a young man paralyzed
In the consciousness of a young man paralyzed
In his need for action and self assertion and who can see
In his need for action and self assertion and who can see
No possibility of action other than the annihilation of
No possibility of action other than the annihilation of
Everything and everyone he sees so that a new heaven
Everything and everyone he sees so that a new heaven
And a new earth may be born so that the new may be
And a new earth may be born so that the new may be
Announced and the old may perish and himself
Announced and the old may perish and himself
The sacrificial instrument—the Christ—through which
The sacrificial instrument—the Christ—through which
These long-desired things may be accomplished.
These long-desired things may be accomplished.

.

How do we mourn
The culture the values the world
That makes all this
A possibility.

for two voices, spoken as a round

FOR IVAN ARGÜELLES UPON HIS COMPLETION
OF ONE HUNDRED SONNETS

"none is greater than the breath
that lingers above the mouth a year and many more a soul
linked to nothing but its other in name only a *sound*"

A *little* sound, a sonnet
One hundred sonnets sitting on a wall
One hundred sonnets ready to take on the entire Petrarchan tradition
Four lines four lines three lines three lines

Argüelles is like Petrarch like Sydney like Spenser like Shakespeare like Berryman
Like thousands of others taking on the son-
Net (David Bromige made a poem about his child and, though it was not fourteen
    lines,
Called it a son-net)

Congrats on the C note to the Bard of la calle Walnut
He has survived deaths in his time
He has made a great moan out of music

He has looked Death in the face and told it,
Thou art nothing but the great Enigma, Oblivion
I have long sought thee in my soul, and I care naught what thou dost.

Thou, dust.

MY APPEARANCE ON *THE ED SULLIVAN SHOW*
(JUNE 6, 1955)

There I am at sweet fifteen
On the television screen
Singing in my baritone
"You Will Never Walk Alone"
As well as that "Beyond the Blue
Horizon" that we had to chew.
When the choir went off pitch
One soprano fixed the hitch
Hitting the exact right note,
Keeping all of us afloat.
Childhood on the TV screen
Flickers at me—there's a scene!
Many of the names have fled
(Many of them now are dead)
But there we all are—lively, noisy,
A thrill for me, born in New Joisey,
A kid my parents (not the stork)
Brought to live in old New York.
Dear Port Chester, Way Back East,
Not the Best, but not the Least.
There I learned to break my tether:
Now I have much better weather.

ISLAND

"NO MAN IS AN ISLAND . . ."

I am the remains
Of an extinct volcano
That reaches 541 feet
Above sea level.
I am situated
Northwest of the main
Galápagos Island group
On the Wolf-Darwin
Lineament.
My formation
Is different from
The formation of the main
Galápagos Islands.
Currently
There are two theories
Of my formation:
The first is that
Magma rising from the mantle plume
Forming the main
Galápagos Islands
Was channeled towards
The Galápagos
Spreading Center;
Alternatively,
There was a separate
Rise in magma caused by stress in the ocean lithosphere
By a transform fault.
I am satisfied.
I am the most northerly
Of the two peaks on the Wolf Darwin Lineament.
My last eruption
Is believed to have been
400,000 years ago.
My Arch is unmatched
By any created in the Ancient World.
I am not open to land visits.
I teem
With a spectacular variety of marine life.
I attract:
Whale sharks, hammerhead, Galápagos, silky and blacktip sharks,
Green turtles, manta rays, and dolphins.
I have a large bird population,
Including frigate birds, red-footed boobies, and the vampire finch.
I love the water out of which I rise.

My heart is open
To the wind, to the elements, to the creatures that visit.
I do not make love.
I do not make war.
I do not believe in any deity.
I stand
In the midst of the magnificent Pacific Ocean
Alive, old, free.

LES DÉFUNTS

Importun
La lune
Vent qui rage!
Ne garde
Les défunts?
Aucune
Ça voyage.
Rancune

They move
The moon
With the wind
Stood shining
These dead ones
Against the blue sky
Scarcely more than
This afternoon
A day in one place
In purity of manifestation
Then on to another
Purity of moon
One moment
And sky
Tallahassee
No rancor
The next
Aucune
Vermont
Rancune

Les défunts?
No bitterness
Ça voyage.

And we go with them
Only the cold sweet light
Nous,
Of human
Tous les morts
Dreams

BELOW THE STATUE, DUFFY SQUARE, NYC:

Once there was a man my father knew
in the old times
when the old century was new
as this new century is new
and the power of him stands
shining in a changed time
amid the immense
bustle of New York City life—
all that grieving joyous murderous life that circumambulates
his poised and elegant presence

as he holds but does not lean upon

his cane

He was my father's mentor and his friend

He lives in the midst
Of the city he loved
Home of the changing Irish,

Standing at exactly the point
At which the Irish redefined themselves
Into something other than
The brawling drunkards
The world defined them as.
They conquered New York
With their lilt and laughter
And their shuffle-ball-change—
And my grandfather,
Big Tom of Tammany,
Died a poor man though he made money
And gave his name to Foley Square.

COHAN DIXIT:

Well, you never know
Where the great ones go
Or even the little ones
So that's Jack Foley's grandson
A grandson Jack Foley never met
And there's Foley's son, another Jack,
Blubbering away at the sight
Of our conjunction:
My mighty presence
(Though all in stone)

And the big smile on the grandson's face
Giving my regards
And his father's
And his grandfather's
To Broadway
(After a proper visit to Saint Pat's).
And isn't it a grand thing
To be alive
And to know these things live
Long after the mortification
Of ourselves.
Song became statue
When I died.
My spirit flew in the air
To its true home
Amid the traffic
Amid the lives
That swirl
In the great city
Where the marvelous Irish made their mark
So many years ago.
Sláinte
And good luck to the Foleys
As they too make their way
Through this infinite vale
Of joy, luck and tears—
Tears sometimes for joy, sometimes for sorrow.

THREE FOR SEAN & KERRY

CHANGING SAUDI ARABIA:
ART, CULTURE AND SOCIETY IN THE KINGDOM
(LYNNE RIENNER PUBLISHERS, 2019)

In these days
Of reading
Electronically
When time
Is in our fingertips
What use
Is a book—OIC
Old fashioned
Informational
Contrivance—
What use
Is something
You can hold
In your hand
Like a lover's
Hand
Or a child's—
What use
Is the feel
Of paper?
It reminds
Us of the world
Which we hold to
So often
With our hands
And not
Our fingertips,
Which we grip
With love
And determination
Which we grip
With love
And determination
And so today,
When my son's
Second published book
Arrived,
It was as if
I held him once again
When he was scarcely bigger
Than this book,

And like this book
He grew
Not only in my mind
But in the world
And now,
At nearly forty-five
(Taller than I),
He has produced
A wonderful contribution
To thinking
To thought itself
As he views
The comedians
Of Saudi Arabia
And speaks
Of Ezra Pound.
Adelle and I
Gave him something
But he found more
And all of it
Arrived today
And is cradled
Not in my arms
But in my hands,
In my mind,
And heart.

UPON SEAN'S BIRTHDAY, UPON THE PUBLICATION
OF HIS SECOND BOOK

Yesterday, three old friends—
Ivan Argüelles, Neeli Cherkovski and I,
Poets all—
Lunched at a Chinese restaurant.
"Old" in both senses—
Age and duration of friendship—
Each of the friends
Had difficulty walking, but
The difficulty differed in each case
So they looked
Like a comedy act out of the 1930s.
They talked about art, old friends,
Kin. Ivan spoke of
His son Alexander's decoration
Of his brother Max's coffin—
Magical script from how many ancient languages,
Turning the coffin into an amazing, sacred object
As it entered the flame.
I told them of your equally amazing new book,
Appearing in time for your birthday
As you turn (!) 45.
So many years ago that person called me "da-eee"
And now he is Dr. Foley.
My father would have loved to have seen it:
Vaudevillian Grandsires Respected Prof!
Hearts bursting with love,
Adelle and I listened to your calls
To tell us of the book's progress.
I don't see how that love can vanish.
Your mother carried it to the end of her days
And perhaps beyond.
I carry it too, and so do you
As we enter this new world,
This new century,
And you, my dear son,
Travel towards fifty.
Our love is with you,
I hope strengthening you,
To the end, even the end,
Of your days.

FOR SEAN AND KERRY IN NASHVILLE

Closer to midnight there
As the dark moves towards
First light of the new year,
As I saw Sean's eyes
First open to see the world
Long, still vivid years ago,
And I think of you both
Safe in a world you know
And that welcomes you
Even as the dark gathers
And the light comes
Once again
And the year opens.
May love and light
Follow you both
As you face
The deep chiaroscuro
Of life on this flawed,
Spinning,
Magnificent
Globe
Throbbing in a galaxy
Which will one day
Vanish
As everything vanishes
Into time
And memory.
Held
In a poem,
In a spinning
Life.

A DUET FOR CHANA BLOCH (FLORENCE INA FAERSTEIN) 1940–2017

Unblessed in a downburst, I lost
Dear Chana,
My leafy summer, my lovely,
Gallant in the struggle
My crest, my crown.
Against what we all struggle against: Death.

I sleep in a flannel nightcap.
Bronx lady,
My wig sleeps in a closet,
Born in my year,
Comb and brush in a drawer.
Your voice carried the Bronx with you wherever you went.

"God blessed you with curly hair,"
"Roger Fogelman, oh yes,
my mother used to say
I remember him"
and dressed me like Shirley Temple.
(Cornell: 58 – 60s)

I wake to a still life—
Fogelman: A vast, unsuccessful crush on your sister, Debbie,
a clock that marks the hour
Ended up, not surprisingly, institutionalized
before it strikes.
Where he continued his practice of formal verse.
        (He had been a formal lover: "Deborah, will you kiss me?" "No.")

No skull on my desk.
You praised my love for my wife.
Just a face in the mirror,
So many praise you now
unrecognizable.
And the love you gave.

—Take these lines from a poet you loved
(And whom I love too)

As you enter that dark place,
That nothing,

Take George Herbert with you,
Easter Wings as you vanish:

My tender age in sorrow did beginne;
  My tender age in sorrow did beginne;
And still with sicknesses and shame
  And still with sicknesses and shame
Thou didst so punish sinne,
  Thou didst so punish sinne,
That I became
  That I became
Most thinne.
  Most thinne.
With Thee
  With Thee
Let me combine,
  Let me combine,
And feel this day Thy victorie;
  And feel this day Thy victorie;
For, if I imp my wing on Thine,
  For, if I imp my wing on Thine,
Affliction shall advance the flight in me.
  Affliction shall advance the flight in me.

ARTAUD

Before speaking further about culture, I must remark that the world is hungry and not concerned with culture, and that the attempt to orient toward culture thoughts turned only toward hunger is a purely artificial expedient.

What is most important, it seems to me, is not so much to defend a culture whose existence has never kept a man from going hungry, as to extract, from what is called culture, ideas whose compelling force is identical with that of hunger.

We need to live first of all; to believe in what makes us live and that something makes us live—to believe that whatever is produced from the mysterious depths of ourselves need not forever haunt us as an exclusively digestive concern.

I mean that if it is important for us to eat first of all, it is even more important for us not to waste in the sole concern for eating our simple power of being hungry.

If confusion is the sign of the times, I see at the root of this confusion a rupture between things and words, between things and the ideas and signs that are their representation.

Not, of course, for lack of philosophical systems; their number and contradictions characterize our old French and European culture: but where can it be shown that life, our life, has ever been affected by these systems? I will not say that philosophical systems must be applied directly and immediately: but of the following alternatives, one must be true:

Either these systems are within us and permeate our being to the point of supporting life itself (and if this is the case, what use are books?), or they do not permeate us and therefore do not have the capacity to support life (and in this case what does their disappearance matter?).

He walks in the spectacle
He was so handsome, très beau, vous savez
that is everything around him
And then . . . et puis après . . . maigre . . . misère
Madly insisting on his
sanity and insanity
SCREAMING and insistent
that he is right
while knowing that he is in excess
and comic and *wrong*—
ironic, sincere,
and vastly accusatory
At once frail and full of authority
"Le *mômo*" qui *joue* le *mômo* pour ses amis artistiques de Paris
DON'T CURE ANYONE OF ANYTHING

CURING PEOPLE IS DEATH
DOCTORS ARE KILLERS
SCIENCE IS BLACK MAGIC
SCIENTISTS ARE BLACK MAGICIANS
WHOSE TOOLS ARE MADNESS AND ELECTRIC SHOCK
AND **PAIN!**

J'ai appris hier

(il faut croire que je retarde, ou peut-être n'est-ce qu'un faux bruit, l'un de ces sales ragots comme il s'en colporte entre évier et latrines à l'heure de la mise aux baquets des repas une fois de plus ingurgités),

j'ai appris hier

l'une des pratiques officielles les plus sensationnelles des écoles publiques américaines

et qui font sans doute que ce pays se croit à la tête du progrès.

Il paraît que parmi les examens ou épreuves que l'on fait subir à un enfant qui entre pour la première fois dans une école publique, aurait lieu l'épreuve dite de la liqueur séminale ou du

SPERME . . .

mo to ho he ah

mem zi ag oh toog

mama

mama

mômo mômo mômo

et moi . . . toothless . . . addicted . . . mem zi ag oh toog

zi zi

BRUCE CONNER: *COSMIC RAY*

for Beth Pewther

the whole ten years of the 60s
the whole ten years of the 60s
in 6
in 6
minutes
minutes
Beth, as you flicker
Beth, as you flicker
& glow
& glow
in the amazing coruscations
in the amazing coruscations
of the phallic
of the phallic

imagination

*

Did you see the death's head in *The Black Dahlia*
Or only the naked woman?
Did you see the low-hanging *cojones*
Of Rudolph Valentino?
Did you see
The hands of the Angel?

*

BLACK DAHLIA

a long assemblage
made to hang from a string
a nude woman
into whose image
the artist has driven nails
the nails suggest the theme
nothing less than a crucifixion

it is Conner's own
life-cry of pain
that one senses
in this *thing*
neither painting nor sculpture
that hangs on a wall

which is as black as it is
"a fiery consciousness
of human injustice"
"monumental
& extremely
shocking"

the society we have
says Conner
is alienating
to the animal
to the animals
we are
to the beasts
that shelter
in our
core

. . .

    Lingering in the Kansas night
    Is a little boy
    With large eyes
    Who listens
    To the deep
    Violations
    Of the turning
    Stars

MAHAGONNY 2018

(variations on Bertolt Brecht's great opera libretto)

Shine,
    green
moon of Alabama
light the way!

We'll get
MONEY
when they come
to Mandalay
when these migrants come to
Mahagonny
where anything goes
Give me
money
says the bar
named Mandalay—(Money
is Sex Appeal)—

. . .

The great, dead Cities
drain us
This
Mahagonny
is only
because everything's rotten

because there's no peace
and no harmony
and nothing
on which
you can rely

. . .

Look at those birds: lovers
circling
you came from Havana
years ago
I came from Alaska
I, Jimmy—
Seven years in the cold
in the snow-covered woods
I made it

and spent it—
now there's nothing left of me

. . .

WE DON'T NEED
HURRICANES
WE DON'T NEED
TYPHOONS
WE CAN DO
WHATEVER THEY DO
BETTER—
    CAPITALISM!

. . .

don't let them fool you
    it's the business
you don't come back
    of the future
day's in the doorway
    to be
but you feel   .
    dangerous
the night wind

.

there's nothing but life
    I first heard it over fifty years ago
you stand with the beasts
    "ein mensch ist kein tier"
they'll use you if you let them
    At seventy eight, I hear it again,
        Lenya's growly, inimitable voice

        the night wind moves me to tears

WHEN THE WONDERFUL MAUDE MAGGART SINGS,

"The River Is So Blue"—
"The River Is So Blue"—
a song dropped from *Blockade* (1938),
a song dropped from Blockade *(1938)*
the film for which it was intended
the film for which it was intended
(which achieved a total loss of $135,672.00)—
(which achieved a total loss of $135,672.00)— one feels the depths
one feels the depths
not of the river
not of the river
but of the song's deeply divided composer, Kurt
but of the song's deeply divided composer, Kurt
Weill,
Weill,
whose music simultaneously
whose music simultaneously
asserts and contradicts
asserts and contradicts
Ann Ronell's faintly banal lyrics ("And you must be mine")
Ann Ronell's faintly banal lyrics ("And you must be mine")
(though she also wrote the wonderful "Willow Weep for Me").
(though she also wrote the wonderful "Willow Weep for Me").

Was the title "The River Is So Blue" suggested by Weill
Was the title "The River Is So Blue" suggested by Weill
as "Speak Low" was suggested to Ogden Nash?
as "Speak Low" was suggested to Ogden Nash?
One remembers, from Weill's German period,
One remembers, from Weill's German period,
"Ja, das Meer ist blau, so blau,"
"Ja, das Meer ist blau, so blau,"
in which the blue beauty of the sea disguises
in which the blue beauty of the sea disguises
the awful fact of the drowned—
the awful fact of the drowned—
and thinks that Weill must have remembered it too.
and thinks that Weill must have remembered it too.
(And the composer returns to the river in his final, unfinished
(And the composer returns to the river in his final, unfinished
Huckleberry Finn.)
Huckleberry Finn.)
Listening to the marvelous Maude Maggart
Listening to the marvelous Maude Maggart the slightly abrasive sweetness of her
voice

the slightly abrasive sweetness of her voice
the extraordinary expressiveness
the extraordinary expressiveness
of her sometimes wavering sense of pitch
of her sometimes wavering sense of pitch
the magnificent moment when she sings, "Ah, love,"
the magnificent moment when she sings, "Ah, love,"
one recognizes
one recognizes
what Hannah Arendt—six years younger than Weill
what Hannah Arendt—six years younger than Weill
but like Weill, German—
but like Weill, German—
called
called
a broken will
a broken will
a will which wills and
a will which wills and
wills not
wills not
at the same time—
at the same time—
which is hardly the Triumph of the Will—
which is hardly the Triumph of the Will—
a will which moves like the river
a will which moves like the river
like Maude Maggart's voice
like Maude Maggart's voice
like the piano accompaniment that suggests the movement of water
like the piano accompaniment that suggests the movement of water
into the indefinite definite
into the indefinite definite
into the impossible possible
into the impossible possible
into the chaos
into the chaos
when the great god Amor
when the great god Amor
turns his eyes
turns his eyes
to the frail human
to the frail human
who listens and obeys.
who listens and obeys.

KING DEATH

King Death sat with The Maiden
Drinking mead
Death said I have seen you often
With the other maidens
Playing amid the flowers
I wonder whether you might play here

O no said The Maiden
To play here one must cross the dark river
Pass by the dog
And be judged
I am too young for all that
There is no gray in my hair
And my voice carries across the field
My voice carries clearly across the field

Listen said the King
Do you hear anyone speaking
Do you hear even an echo of a voice
Speak again

And she did. There was nothing
Not even an echo

You have crossed the dark river
Said the King
You have become one with the wind
And the sun
And the bright, dying, obedient, matchless stars
And the vast, bright, dying, obedient stars

BLINDNESS & INSIGHT

There are things we don't know
    There are things we don't know
about what we know
    about what we know
There is an element
    There is an element
of ignorance in the midst of our deepest gnosis
    of ignorance in the midst of our deepest gnosis
Woody Guthrie, obsessed
    Woody Guthrie, obsessed
by Lead Belly's song, "Goodnight, Irene"—
    by Lead Belly's song, "Goodnight, Irene"— and no doubt by Lead Belly—
    and no doubt by Lead Belly—
reproduced that tune
    reproduced that tune
in a number of his own compositions:
    in a number of his own compositions:
he didn't know
    he didn't know
until someone told him,
    until someone told him,
"Woody, you done it again"
    "Woody, you done it again"
A friend, a deeply self-aware poet,
    A friend, a deeply self-aware poet,
wrote "dark" into almost all his poems
    wrote "dark" into almost all his poems
until he was made aware of it
    until he was made aware of it
What word is he repeating now?
    What word is he repeating now?
Another poet friend
    Another poet friend
is obsessed by "blue"
    is obsessed by "blue"
which appears
    which appears
more than any other color word
    more than any other color word
in her work
    in her work
Is it the color of the Virgin Mary
    Is it the color of the Virgin Mary
the sky

                the sky
the "blues"?
                the "blues"?
Half-noticing perhaps
                Half-noticing perhaps
she titled an entire section of her book,
                she titled an entire section of her book,
"Pink"
                "Pink"
There are these words
                These are the words
that haunt us—"haints"—
                that haunt us—"haints"—
no matter what we write
                no matter what we write
no matter the subject
                no matter the subject
If we could read them
                If we could read them
we might know ourselves
                we might know ourselves
as others know us
                as others know us
but all we do
                but all we do
is write them down
                is write them down
over and over again
                over and over again
"Blindness and Insight,"
                "Blindness and Insight,"
wrote Paul de Man
                wrote Paul de Man
in a marvelous moment
                in a marvelous moment
of blind insight
                of blind insight
What did he fail to see when he saw
                What did he fail to see when he saw
the negative element
                the negative element
at the center
                at the center
of consciousness
                of consciousness
the black hole

> *the black hole*
which captures light
> *which captures light*
but will not
> *but will not*
set it
> *set it*
free
> *free*

FREEWAY INCIDENT

as I drove the poet Argüelles home yesterday
(the poet Barbara Guest said to me, "You have always known how to free your
    mind")
we saw, by the side of the freeway,
on a little hillock,
a dead deer
(you have always known how to free your mind)
beautiful, young, a female
Argüelles and I had been talking
about Death and Grief and how the mind
denies, accepts, denies, accepts
(you have always known how to free your mind)
the immense fact of obliteration—
though it is a mystery
and a terror:
as we drove I said, "Look"
and there Death was
beautiful, young,
almost as if sleeping (though we knew better),
like an image from a painting or a film
and we spoke a little and drove on
(you have always known how to free your mind)
beyond the dead deer
beyond our conversation
(you have always known how to free your mind)
and vicious night began (endlessly) to fall

THE DARK ONE

Thank the lord for the word eternity
For the word death
For the word love
These may be wordlings only
This may be a mode
Of the fabulous untruth
Underlying everything
Words allow us to live
In World
The Christ
Scatters us
Not into truth
But into unfathomable enigma
He will never return
Never that body again
But he lives in our minds
Because he escapes not death
But category.
. . .
Unknown and non-existent,
God of the rebus, of the puzzle,
Of the unknowable outcome:
God of the Word

FOR JULIA
FOR THE MARVELOUS, LAUDED STREET POET OF
TELEGRAPH AVENUE

Julia,
Of the bright and dark
Streets of this West,
This Berkeley,
I think of you this night
Of the phantom full moon
And the skulls and heads
And black clothes
That make you look
Like a perpetual Halloween.
Julia,
Of the bubbles, the quick wit,
The half smile,
The way with a phrase,
"This was a lady
Trying to be
A machine,"
Of the famous limp,
The resilience,
The courage,
The ability to turn fools,
Skewered, into a line of verse,
The deep, light laughter,
The slight touch of gray showing beneath the hat,
The seller of your own
Vast Volumes,
The laughing eyes—
You fill my mind this night of your sickness
This night when your studied, careful independence
Is no longer possible,
And I think of the many poets
Who have entered hospitals
Who have been tended, not read,
Placed in the care of hands
That do not open books
But close
And suture
The wounds life visits upon us all
As we sit in this café of many entrances
But only one exit
And sip our lattes, our cappuccinos, our espressos, our macchiatos
And talk and dream—

And smoke—

On a street that dreams
It is not a street
But Life.

. . .

I visited Julia tonight. She was lying on the bed in her room. "Hi, Jack." Without her Julia costume—particularly without her hat—she didn't look like the Julia I think of. But the moment she smiled, Julia was back. That smile—warm, with sometimes just a trace of irony—is definitively Julia. There were a couple of moments where she was just a little vague, but for the most part, as Jan Steckel says, "she's still her." I brought her a funny toy: a black cat with some orange clothes—her colors—that chattered when you pushed it and said, "Happy Halloween." "That's the silliest thing I've ever seen," she said, smiling. I agreed with her. I told her how and what I've been doing. She listened with interest and made pleased comments when I showed her photographs of Sangye and me. I told her of my deep grief for Adelle and how I had wanted to die—and how Sangye had changed so much of that. She said, twice, "I understand that." She told me that the doctors didn't tell her much about her condition and that the food was "hospital food." She put her thumb down. I asked her whether she were writing and she answered somewhat enigmatically, "It's different." I think she meant that the conditions were different. I told her I would bring her a big pad and some pens. She said, emphatically, "That would help!" She pointed out the paintings Debbie had done which decorated her room. I mentioned that Debbie had painted Julia often. Julia nodded and said, "Yes, she has." I added that I thought Debbie's portrait of her on the cover of the new book, *Between the Cracks*, was particularly fine. She was pleased by that. I also told her how much I liked the new book. She said, sincerely not "politely," "That's good to hear." I told her about the radio show I was planning and mentioned that David Gollub had written a very nice poem about her. She answered quietly, "He would." I promised that I would bring her some pens and a big pad of paper—but she had to promise to write something in the pad. Julia's unfailing elegance of manner and her quiet good humor manifested even in these difficult circumstances. It was a very nice visit. I told her how old I was. She said, "You have a few years on me, not many." I explained that I lived quite close by and had a car. If she needed something, I could probably supply it. I went off to try a nearby Chinese restaurant, Ark. One of the dishes I had was superb: wonderful, juicy pork dumplings. I got two extra orders of them, one for Sangye and one for Julia. When I finished my meal, I went to Walgreens and bought a big pad of paper and some pens. I went back to Park Bridge Nursing Home with my treasures. Julia seemed happy to see me and graciously accepted the gifts. When I told her I was giving her the wonderful pork dumplings as an antidote to hospital food, she smiled and gave me a thumbs up. (Yes, I know she's Jewish.) Then the nurse came in to administer a shot of insulin. I said goodbye for now and drove home. Julia is still very much alive.

11/3/18

FOR JULIA VINOGRAD (12/11/43 - 12/5/18)

Can a street mourn?
Can a street shed tears?
How many of them gone now?
Julia shedding her street persona
Shedding everything—body, friends, paraphernalia of life
Gone now with Jack Micheline, Gene Ruggles, poets
Hawking their wares on the streets of Berkeley and everywhere,
Leaving their words here, there, everywhere.
(In the nursing home) "I miss your hat."
"So do I." (Gesturing) "It's behind me."
Deep with the first dead lies Berkeley's daughter
Another woman gone
To the deep grains of our hearts.

12/5/18

. . .

AFTER THE MEMORIAL

Like everyone else, I found the memorial a wonderful, moving event. "Perfect," as Jan Steckel put it. As with the event honoring Al Young, we demonstrated that for all our divisions, dislikes, snobbery, etc., we were also a community, people that can come together in a way that honors our own. Julia could, I suppose, be difficult and divisive, but I never experienced such things with her. I always felt respect and affection on both our sides. I was always glad to see her—and to hear her. She was an elegant presence in what was sometimes a crazy scene—a scene she loved for its very madness. She said of my work, early on, when not everyone understood it at all, "You're the only person I know who does Esoteric Vaudeville." I loved the comment and loved that she loved vaudeville—which was probably another name for the places she haunted, the Café Babar most of all. We'll all miss her, but I can't imagine poetry in this area without her. Goodbye, you elegant, ironic, talented lady. I'll miss your poetry—and I'll miss your hats.

. . .

MEMORIAL

Julia wore death
every day of her life
She wore death
until death came
to claim her
Jerusalem
opening herself
to the father god
Julia wore black
until blackness
surrounded her
and we came to sing her praises
and to weep
and laugh
we sang blackness
back to the father,
sang her death
in the big room
in Oakland,
California
where Julia was not
because she had already
abandoned the earth
so many people!
so many stories!
I stayed,
Jerusalem,
until tears came
and I could not stay
more
and I saw your image
radiant
in the dark rain
of that rainy day

1/6/19

DAFFODIL / ASPHODEL

Daffodil
Who has their flowers
Is Asphodel
The dead ones
Flower
Food
Of the dead
Echoes
The great meadow
Words meld—
Covered with the yellow flower
Williams?
Did Wordsworth know?
Wordsworth?
Surely Williams did
Yellow its color
The words meld &
The great meadow
Echo
Of the dead
Food
Flowers:
For the dead ones
Asphodel:
Who have their flowers
Daffodils

WIND

As he died he was surprised to discover
That he had become the wind
Not in the sense of *Spiritus*
But the wind
That has to do with flowers, dust, wildness,
And the world,
Is gentle at times
But also furious and angry,
Even murderous,
Though also kindly and supportive of life.
He had left behind
What bound him to the earth
And had become
Boundless.
Slowly, his consciousness
Vanished.

    for Stephen Cole

BY MARK FISHER:

I boarded the same ship
Kerouac sailed back from Paris on

I was shy of five

my first memory a daydream

falling into the Atlantic

rescued by dolphins

what did I know about dolphins at that tender age

true story

. . .

JACK'S RESPONSE:

we tell stories
but nothing in a poem is true

things happen
and we speak of them

but words are fictions
no matter how much we pretend

otherwise

dolphins carry the souls of the dead
to the happy isles

when you were a child
one gazed at you and said,
I will return for you, child,

after the flood of years

THE DOMINION OF LIGHT

am I the only one who knows
how much
you loved that painting

for Adelle
. . .
DEAR GHOST,

. . . If I could believe
That your spirit
Lives on
I would rejoice
Boundlessly
But—as you knew—
I always found
The Bible's great definition of faith,
"The substance of things hoped for,
The evidence of things not seen,"
To be a definition of wish, of fiction
Of, at its extreme, delusion—
And so I remain
An irreligious man
A man of the darkness
Whose only light
Lies in this world,
Where you came
And cared for me
And loved me
And vanished with the wind.

BY PETER N. SHERBURN-ZIMMER:

The moon is my mistress, but she is there for everyone.
Her light may not be her own
but . . . like the fallen leaf . . .
she too belongs in the winter lake.

JACK'S ANSWER:

In the lake, the moon.
On the shore, so many leaves
Falling as I look.

SEA BREEZE

The flesh is sad, alas! and I've read all the books.
To run away—to run away *down there*. I feel that birds are drunk
They want to be in unknown foam and skies!
Nothing—not even the gardens reflected in your eyes—
Will hold this heart that drenches in the sea—
Ah, nights!—not even the desolate brilliance of the lamp by which I see
The empty paper whose white-
Ness defends it, nor the young wife
With her child suckling: I'm leaving—
Weigh anchor!—going to a place where there is no grieving.
An immense Boredom—thrust from hope to griefs—
Believes still in the supreme goodbye of waving handkerchiefs! . . .

And perhaps the masts will summon storms
That blast the sails and wreck the oars:
Lost, without sail, without sail, or beating oars . . .
But oh, my heart, listen to the song of *sailors*.

Stéphane Mallarmé (1865)

WHEN SLEEP COMES

JACK FOLEY: 79 (AUGUST 9, 2019)

7 KEYS TO JACK FOLEY

1. He is Irish.

2. He is Italian.

3. He is Irish and Italian.

4. He is Irish and Italian and writes poetry.

5. He is Irish and Italian and writes poetry and talks a lot.

6. He is Irish and Italian and a Californian and writes poetry and talks a lot.

7. He is Irish and Italian and a Californian and writes poetry and talks a lot and has wonderful friends who make him pictures and write him poems and wish him a happy birthday as he enters the hallowed halls of Antiquity with a leap and a bound and a tendency towards transgressive behavior. And what continent will you be in, Mr. Foley? I am likely to be in INcontinent. Heh. 79. Years flew. Still flying.

LATIN / WHEN SLEEP COMES

Latin is the lesson we were taught
Antiquity still living in a "dead" language
I grew up with it as the language of the church
Made sense of it with the help of a little book, a "missal"
As the priest intoned.
Later, I learned Caesar, Virgil
The long vowels rising up in the deep cadence of the line
Arma Virumque Cano
The labor it was to found Rome
All that history embodied in sounds
Dido mad and loving
The soldier turning away from passion
Carthago delenda est
Rome
Founded,
Rome
The home of the Catholic Church
The home of a history I had no part of
But which somehow defined me
The arguments of theologians
The Church Triumphant
Heavenly City / Earthly City
Passion, triumph
Perhaps the last gasp of Spirit
Carthago delenda est
How do we become
Most blessed
How are we
Sanctified in this scramble
Is renunciation the answer
Forgive me, father
Mea culpa
Mea maxima culpa
My sins are unknown except to thee
My tears
My history of ill.
In the last hour
Give me strength
To let it all go
To let me die
Like a language
Unspoken
For centuries
Like Latin

Like the Rome of Virgil
Like Carthage
Like, soon perhaps, the Catholic Church
In the vast ruin
Of historical circumstance
And the whirl
Of time—

when sleep comes
    sleep comes
if it comes
    until
when sleep comes
    until
dream
    as we live our lives
or dreamless
    day by day
gain new strength
    that follows us
when sleep comes
    abyss
set mind free
    ocean of darkness
(if it comes)
    drift
drift
    set mind free
ocean of darkness
    when sleep comes
abyss
    gain new strength
that follows us
    or dreamless
day by day
    dream
as we live our lives
    when sleep comes
until
    if it comes
until
    when sleep comes
sleep comes

In the amazing
Passage
From the dark
To the dark
We discover
Nothing but life
How did we ever
Get so old?
Springs and summers
Winters and falls
All pass by
As we watch
And learn
To listen to the wind
That whispers,
Evanescence,
Mindfulness,
Love.
Evanescence,
Mindfulness,
Love.

Mr. Death, he comes knocking at the door

APPENDIX

COLLABORATIVE PRAISEPOEM FOR AL YOUNG

suggested & orchestrated by Jack Foley
written by 35 poets

In April of 1965 I enjoyed the first of a remarkable and continuing series of (non-drug-induced) mystical experiences that I consider, thus far, to be the high points of my life. I no longer feel compelled, as I once did, to speak of these experiences directly. I have learned quite painfully that most people are not especially eager to hear of such things, and many, in fact, feel threatened or frightened by them.

—Al Young

For me the writing of poetry is a spiritual activity. Poetry should be the music of love: song, a dance, the joyously heartbreaking flight of the human spirit through inner and outer space in search of itself.

—Al Young

I Am Not Only Witty In Myself, But The Cause That Wit Is In Other Men.

—Falstaff, *Henry IV, Part Two*

If Al Young were a baseball team, he'd win the World's Series.

—Anon

Al Young is great
He is a star, radiating love
and creativity into our lives.
His southern drawl, his use of language, his style, and coolness. Let us open the door
and be charmed.
Al's words are bullet-proof.
Al is great for sharing his jumping for Spring attitude with every joyful breath he takes.

An O B G
(oldie but
goodie)

I

Al

together, listening in silence
What keeps Al young
despite the gray?
That irrepressible
sense of play.
Al is great
Al is choice
Al writes poetry
that illuminates
with a gentle light
and a passionate voice
He's the laureate
of everywhere

FOR AL YOUNG, READING HIS POEMS AGAIN

He stands before me

like a gentle giant

going back in time

new promise of a deepness

a mystery his words

unfold

I hear from Sidney J. Prettymon that the world and its songs,
as sung by Al Young, is so alive
you'd almost think you knew where Angelina is.
I call him Mr. Suede, a gentle man of letters.
Life, like ice, can be hard, cold but Al, arms outstretched, skates.
What a treat to be
Al Young and look
into a mirror!
Al Young is great
the way the day is great
it begins in glory and cedes unto night
as the sun grows dark, still glowing, still great.
As the air is great, preserving time for music.
He weren't goin' down that big road by his-self
he wus goin' with them angels and they was blowin' the blues.
Each day our hands discover
the blue-emerald river heart
we dive into its clear pool
spirit laughing our river current.
Al's voice sings a long rich jazz note, deep and smooth,
of all the places he touches on in this world and loves well
Al is the music of the Blue Train, the quiet in my cupped palms, the voice dreaming
    my past.
his warm welcome tied to universal love, his full expression of a shared humanity
    unabated
by any other music, and it's there right away, every time, every time
On the #18, AC Transit bus
Al and I chat poetry
A young woman listening
Speaks up tentatively
Al invites her in,
She & I his equal

His heart that big.

I love Al Young's voice, his generous way of being in the world.

His body of work I trust will always be read.

From *Drowning in the Sea of Love,* Al's own words: "How could you ever let a song go
out of your heart, when you are already song? O the beautiful changes!"

Young Al Young
found Al found Mingus
a memoir, or two.

poems that light up the mind
like a field of fire flies
lingering images that haunt the mind
like a restless ghost
Space inside a poem
Was smaller before you came
With the muse at home in Al Young's young heart!
In the depth most of darkness
—a sudden light—
as if by magic
When I met his eyes
there was no end to him—
Al is a Master Chef who can manipulate
language and emotion by adding pinches of
rhyme and reason that adds flavor and
seasoning to his Poetry Stew!
Al Young is great is an understatement. Al's
presence in our lives is a reminder of the
divinity living in each of us.
(Sent, with love,
from the Deep South)
his pure energy, a kindly fire, the immediate infinity in his eyes
Al sings "April in Paris" in his poem, all of us brought there by his bluesy words
Al Young, lion with a gentle roar, I salute you!
December: season of gloom the perpetual note sung by Al Young's mellow
voice in low C just below the Delta from which the Dark issues
the words of Al Young
leave no snow prints nor shadow
—the arc of the moth
Here's an acronym for al young:
Always Loving Years Outpouring Unlimited New Graces
. . .

MAY 31 (AL'S BIRTHDAY, WALT'S BIRTHDAY)

Once this day
Belonged only
To our national poet
Whose name means
White Man
Now, another name
To add to this day
A name that says Young
A name that says
African American
A name that says
Yes, we acknowledge Walt
But here, in the middle of his name,
wALt,
Comes AL

CONTRIBUTORS:

"Al Young is great" *Jack Foley*

"He is a star . . . our lives" *Lucille Lang Day*

"His Southern drawl . . . charmed" *Kim McMillon*

"Al's words are bullet-proof" *Cate Gable*

"Al is great . . . breath he takes" *Kevin Patrick Sullivan*

"An OBG . . . listening in silence" *Gary Gach*

"What keeps Al young . . . sense of play" *David Mason*

"Al is great . . . laureate of everywhere" *Jake Berry*

"FOR AL YOUNG, READING . . . unfold" *Jerome Rothenberg, 12/6/18*

"I hear from Sidney . . . Angelina is" *Robert Hass*

"I call him . . . letters" *Floyd Salas*

"Life, like ice . . . skates" *Claire Ortalda*

"What a treat . . . mirror" *Marvin R. Hiemstra*

"Al Young is great . . . time for music" *Kevin Killian*

"He weren't goin' . . . the blues" *Dave Holt*

"Each day our hands . . . river current" *Chris Olander*

"Al's voice sings . . . loves well" *Mary-Marcia Casoly*

"Al is the music . . . my past" *Anita Endrezze*

"On the #18 . . . that big" *Fred Dodsworth*

"his warm welcome . . . every time" *Bobby Coleman*

"I love Al Young's voice . . . always be read" *Kathleen Weaver*

"From *Drowning* . . . beautiful changes" *Bob Baldock*

"Young Al Young . . . or two" *Zigi Lowenberg*

"poems that light up . . . restless ghost" *A.D. Winans*

"Space inside . . . before you came" *Kim Shuck*

"With the Muse . . . heart" *Dan Brady*

"in the depth . . . by magic" *Jake Berry*

"when I met his eyes . . . to him" *Julie Rogers*

"Al is a Master Chef . . . Poetry Stew" *Jemela Mwelu*

"Al Young is great . . . Deep South" *Pam Kingsbury*

"*his pure energy . . . in his eyes*" *Brenda Hillman*

"Al sings . . . words" *Joyce Jenkins*

"Al Young . . . salute you" *Lenore Weiss*

"December: season . . . Dark issues" *Ivan Argüelles*

"the words . . . moth" *Amos White*

"Here's an acronym . . . Graces" *Elizabeth Nisparos*

"MAY 31 . . . comes AL" *Jack Foley*

AFTERWORD & NOTES

This book was written when I was in my late seventies (I was born in 1940). I am in relatively good health, but if you publish a book at the age of 79, you have to allow for the possibility that it might be your last book. I hope more will come, but these poems, selected from a great number written over the past two or three years, represent an emptying: I have no idea what will come next. Seeing my wife Adelle through her death was a harrowing, complex, and still ongoing experience that I tried to explore in my book, *Grief Songs*. Immediately after her death, I wanted to die and, *at the same time*, found myself constantly, vehemently writing. The poems in this book are partly the production of that exercise in vehemence. Going through the process, I found myself thinking of a wonderful phrase from Whitman's "When Lilacs Last in the Dooryard Bloom'd": "Death's outlet song of Life." (Whitman adds in commentary, "for well dear brother I know, / If thou wast not granted to sing thou would'st surely die.") I felt that Whitman's phrase expressed exactly what had been happening to me. It is probably for this reason that his shadow is everywhere in this book—and, probably, in all my books. This is "Holiday Candy":

> I am a Whitman sampler
> *During holidays*
> There is scarcely a line
> *I buy a Whitman Sampler.*
> I have written that does not bear
> *I like the chocolates*
> His signature as well.
> *The varied forms*
> I am a Whitman sampler
> *The singularity*
> I write in a way
> *Of bonbons*
> Only he made possible.
> *I like their*
> Who knew that a poem
> *Darkness*
> Could be an aria?
> *And their sweetness*
> Who knew that speech
> *And the syrup*
> Was song?
> *That emerges from their depths*

Who understood
And besides,
The vast transformative sea
  I am a Whitman Sampler
More than he?
  Too.

Another extraordinary occurrence of this period was my meeting with Sangye Land, about whom much is said in these poems. Sangye and I met on December 28, 2016. A friend of mine and I were visiting Sangye's stepfather, poet David Meltzer, who was on his deathbed. (David died in the early hours of January 1, 2017.) Sangye, the daughter of David's wife, poet Julie Rogers, was orchestrating the visitors. I thought she was absolutely gorgeous. She walked over to me, hand extended, and said, "I don't believe I know you." We had an enchanting conversation. I was dazzled and upon arriving home immediately wrote "50 Designs to Murder Magic." Believing that "there was no way on earth we could be lovers"—she was thirty three, I was seventy seven—I took my title from a book by Antonin Artaud. Nonetheless, I was astonished to discover that, at my age and with the weight of grief upon me, I could feel like that. Romance seemed utterly impossible though, on my side, vehemently desired. Our first date was on Valentine's Day, 2017. We date our relationship from that day. I wrote in a Valentine's Day poem meant to be "light," "I'm seeing paradise / in a pair of human eyes." Life constantly surprises us.

VALENTINE

It's said that Orpheus
Cruelly beheaded
Continued to speak
In a commanding voice
Is not the same thing
True of Valentine?
Is not Valentine
With all his messages
A type
Of Orpheus?
. . .
a violent sweetness stains your day
it will not be swept away
when Amor Vincit Omnia

NOTES

AUTHOR'S INTRODUCTION

Jerome Rothenberg and I were driving, and I put on the recording of Eliot's reading of *The Waste Land*. We listened transfixed. When it ended, Jerry turned to me and said, "Jesus, *The Waste Land* is a great poem." Deny it as we will—and many do—but we were created by that poem. And yes, Ezra Pound, *il miglior fabbro*. Modernism on steroids. But *The Waste Land* goes back to Whitman: "Out of the Cradle Endlessly Rocking" is perhaps even more "Modernist" than *The Waste Land*. Another poem of voices—and a foundation text of American literature. Eliot—no doubt unknowingly—recreates Whitman for a generation that for the most part had lost the capacity to read him.

ELEGY: GOODBYE, BEAT THING

"Beat ephemera . . . ORDEAL": quotations from David Meltzer's book, *Beat Thing* (2004), an affectiocritical encounter with the author's past and with the entire Beat Generation. The concluding lines of my poem are a paraphrase of the concluding lines of Meltzer's poem, "17:ii:82 (Monk)," published in *The Name: Selected Poetry 1973-1983* and in *David's Copy* (2005).

FIRE BRICKS

Bricks from the fire of 1906, though misshapen, were used in the construction of buildings throughout the San Francisco Bay Area. The ones referred to in this poem are at the corner of Oak and Ninth in Oakland. Though misshapen and scarred, they are powerful emblems of resilience and have their own sort of beauty.

JUNE

The performance by Adelle and me on Jack Foley Day in Berkeley was captured on video, which can be seen on my YouTube page.

THE GLOAMING / MEÁCHAN RUDAÍ

This poem is in part a tribute to the great Irish group, The Gloaming. "Meáchan Rudaí" = "The Weight of Things"; it is the stunning opening track of *The Gloaming 3*. The track is a setting of a poem by the Irish poet Liam Ó Muirthile. The English translation is by Gabriel Rosenstock. My soundcloud page (https://soundcloud.com/john-w-foley/) will give you my recitation of my poem and Jake Berry's beautiful performance of his setting of it.

BLURB

This was written as a blurb for Lewis Turco's book, *The Sonnetarium*. Neither Lewis nor any of the other poets (many of them dedicated formalists) to whom I showed the blurb noticed that it was a sonnet—with rhyme and meter. They were evidently defeated by the fact that it was laid out as prose; I suspect that none of them read it aloud.

TENNESSEE, 2018

The DDD Monster is a character in my story, "The Monst," published in *The Tiger and Other Tales* (Sagging Meniscus Press, 2016).

THANKSGIVING NIGHT, 2017

Jake Berry's beautiful setting of this poem is also on SoundCloud.

SANGYE

These lines from my poem, "King Amour," published in my book, *Life* (Word Palace Press, 2014), are relevant to the entire sequence:

> how many hours—lonely—
> spent in parks—on benches—the light fading—looking—
> to fall into the   DELIRIUM
> which we call   love
> is the mind's attempt
> to *know* itself
> not by the way   of reason
> by the way   of   EROS—

GATE, GATE, PARAGATE, PARASAMGATE, BODHI SVAHAA!

My title: Mantra from *The Heart Sutra*. Variously translated. One: "Gone, Gone, Gone beyond, Gone utterly beyond. O what an awakening." The poem glances at the fact that in Tibetan the name Sangye means "Buddha."

EASTER RAIN,

Chants/chance.

ONDINE

After Giraudoux's play (1938). After the film, *The Shape of Water* (2017).

BIRTHDAY POEM FOR SANGYE

The poem perhaps suggests that she was born in Oregon. She wasn't: she was born in Mount Shasta, California, though she was raised in Oregon.

SANGYE AT TASHI CHOLING

Tashi Choling is a center for Buddhist Studies located in Oregon.

CHANSON D'AMOUR ET DE LA LITÉRATURE

In English:

> SONG OF LOVE AND OF LITERATURE
> I have
> All the books of the world
> And all the books
> Say that I love you
> Really?
> Absolutely.
> Scandinavian books?
> Yes, even Scandinavian books
> The books of Germany?
> Yes, the books of Germany
> The books of the Sahara?
> Yes, yes, even these books
> All the books of the world
> Say
> "I love you"
> . . .
> Is this poem for Sangye?
> Absolutely!

LIGHT

I have always had a fondness for "light" verse, and I enjoy writing it. This section was initially thought of as a place where I could print some samples of my light verse, but the "light" kept getting darker as I included various poems. "Rant, After Florida" is clearly the climax of this tendency.

FOR WILLIAM BLAKE'S BIRTHDAY (NOV. 28)

"Blake" is an old form of "black," found in both Chaucer and Skelton. I take it that it functions as a pun in "The Little Black Boy": "And I am BLAKE, but O! my soul is white."

GUIT
ARRA

The spatial arrangement of this shaped poem was done by my friend, the artist Paul Veres.

THREE SONG LYRICS

These song lyrics were written for my songwriter/performer friend, Tony Perez. Tony has already set (and recorded) "Without You" and "Sado With Him." You can hear his work on YouTube and SoundCloud.

LES DÉFUNTS

These lines,

> Importun
> Vent qui rage !
> Les défunts ?
> Ça voyage. . ..
> Troublesome
> Wind that rages!
> The dead?
> They travel. . .

are from Jules Laforgue's poem, "Complainte de l'oubli des morts."

The line, "La lune ne garde aucune rancune" (The moon holds no grudges) is from T.S. Eliot's Laforgue-influenced "Rhapsody on a Windy Night." My line, "Nous, tous les morts" = Us, all the dead.

BELOW THE STATUE, DUFFY SQUARE, NYC

The photo of my son Sean beneath the statue of George M. Cohan was taken by Kerry Foley in December, 2017. Sean, a historian, discovered that Foley Square was very likely named for my grandfather (his great grandfather), "Big Tom" Foley. See http://wecantourthat.com/big-tom-foley. I was married there in 1961, but I didn't know. I recently wrote this about Big Tom:

now I
look back at him
grateful for what he did
in the long years ago
before the Irish
were rich
before they forgot
to care

A DUET FOR CHANA BLOCH (FLORENCE INA FAERSTEIN) 1940–2017

This poem contains lines quoted from Chana Bloch's poem, "Memento Mori," published in *The New Yorker*, Nov. 16, 2015. I have changed the sequence of some of the lines.

ARTAUD

"Before speaking further . . . what does their disappearance matter?" is from *The Theater and Its Double,* translated by Mary Caroline Richards (Grove Press, 1958).

très beau, vous savez = very handsome, you know

et puis après . . . maigre . . . misère = and then afterwards . . . thin, gaunt . . . poverty

le mômo = a term he chose for himself from Marseilles slang: the divine idiot, in some ways the child

"Le mômo" qui joue *le mômo pour ses amis artistiques de Paris* = "The *mômo*" who *plays* the *mômo* for his artistic Parisian friends

mo to, etc. = nonsense syllables of a sort he used to punctuate his poetry

et moi = and I

J'ai appris hier . . . Translation:

I learned yesterday

(I must be behind the times, or perhaps it's only a false☒rumor, one of those pieces of spiteful gossip that are circulated between sink and latrine at the hour when meals that have been ingurgitated one more time are thrown in the slop buckets),

I learned yesterday

one of the most sensational of those official practices of American public schools

which no doubt account for the fact that this country believes itself to be in the vanguard of progress,

It seems that, among the examinations or tests required of a child entering public school for the first time, there is the so-called seminal fluid or sperm test . . .

—from *Pour en finir avec le jugement de dieu* / *To End God's Judgment,* trans. Victor Corti.

SEA BREEZE

This is my translation of Mallarmé's classic 1865 poem, "Brise Marine." Two quotations from Mallarmé:

In "Crise de vers" (1896) Mallarmé writes, "L'oeuvre pure implique la disparition élocutoire du poète, qui cède l'initiative aux mots . . ." ("The pure work implies the disappearance of the poet as speaker, yielding his initiative to words . . .")

"A century ago in Paris, the painter Degas had lamented that his poems weren't any good though his ideas were wonderful, and the poet Mallarmé responded, "But my dear Degas, poems are made of words, not ideas."

Mallarmé's commentators seem not to have noticed the extraordinary pun at the conclusion of "Brise Marine." In the poem's penultimate line, everything is lost ("Perdus"): there are no masts ("mâts") and no isles ("îlots")—they have vanished: "Perdus, sans mâts, sans mâts, ni fertiles îlots . . ." Yet, in a sense, the concluding word, "matelots," gives the poet back the very things he has lost: the *sound* of "matelots" ("sailors") contains "mâts" + "îlots." The "lost" masts and isles are not restored to the poet as entities, only as names, echoing words. *But that is all they were to begin with.* In a way, the proper translation of the concluding line is "But, oh my heart, listen to the song of 'mâts' + 'îlots.'" One can sense in this early poem—written when the author was in his twenties—an extraordinary shift from a focus on "things" to a focus on "words." The poem insists that it is not a description of reality, not even of imagined reality: rather, it is something made out of words, and if you lose something in the context of words—as opposed to the context of reality—then it can be restored through words. *Finnegans Wake* is not all that far from "Brise Marine." If, from one point of view, the poet's fear of action—of actually making the trip announced by the poem—propels him to find refuge in language, from another point of view the poem enunciates a new mode of beauty. My translation attempts to include the pun: sail/oars-sailors. Note also that Mallarmé's penultimate line is only eleven syllables, not twelve. The . . . is the twelfth syllable.

COLLABORATIVE PRAISEPOEM FOR AL YOUNG

This poem was created as part of a celebration of the life and work of poet Al Young, who attended the celebration. I suggested that a collaborative poem would be appropriate and that the opening line should be "Al Young is great." It was a marvelous event. It took place Thursday, December 27 at the San Francisco Public Library's Koret Auditorium. Video of me reading the praisepoem is on YouTube.

. . .

My friend Ed Mycue writes, "WEAVING INTO THE TESTIMONY OF MY WRITING LIFE THESE ODD INCLUSIONS IN VITAMIN 'M' ('M' BEING FOR 'minus') THAT END UP IN THE TAPESTRY YOU SINK BACK INTO AND LIKE A PENELOPE YOU HAVE SPENT ALL THIS LIFETIME WEAVING AND UNWEAVING AS YOU WAIT FOR THE RETURN OF SOME LORD CALLED ULYSSES AND. . ."

I answered: This is lovely, Ed, but I think this "waiting" you mention is the way our expectations of the new manifest in our lives. It's not that Ulysses never comes—though he never comes; it's that he always remains as a possibility, an emblem of what MIGHT happen. Beckett's *Waiting for Godot* is probably the most negative version of this experience but positive versions are also possible. Behind it all, perhaps, in our secularly Christian culture, is the always thwarted hope that Christ may return: "I know that my redeemer liveth" (Job 19). He does, but he doesn't show.

> So we continue, we survivors
> We whose address books
> Fail to keep up with non existence.
> Was, not is, though new names
> Are written, in computers, not books.
> Who knew some people would live so long.
> Who knew some people would not.
> Not us—the dreamy ones
> Whose addresses fail to keep up
> With Life's dark sister
> Though we try, and fail, to allow for her endless, troublesome meddling.

WHY SOME OF MY POEMS REPEAT LINES

People frequently ask me why I repeat lines in some of my poems. I'd like to address that question here.

It has been one of the unfortunate effects of the teaching of poetry that readers have thought of the poem as "saying something," of having "content," though it is content which is, alas, often opaque, hidden, requiring "elucidation." What in the world is the poet trying to say—and why doesn't the poet just say it directly? Of course, poems—even highly "obscure" ones—do have content, so there is some reason for this complaint, but the point I would like to make is that content is not the primary point of the poem: the poem is less a vehicle for communicating thought, ideas ("saying something"), than it is a vehicle for communicating *feeling*. Poems are not supposed to tell us something—we have prose for that: poems are supposed to arouse us. Some of the most famous poems in the world are enormously enigmatic, mysterious—yet they plunge us into a world which is fascinating, moving, even astonishing, "mysterioso," as Thelonious Monk once put it. No one has ever discovered what *Hamlet* is about—why does the title character behave like that?—yet the experience of the play has kept audiences enthralled for centuries. Why does Iago do what he does in *Othello*?

In my case, what is the difference between

> innocence
> matched with
> intelligence
> sweetness
> matched with
> guile

and

> innocence
> > *innocence*
> matched with
> > *matched with*
> intelligence
> > *intelligence*
> sweetness
> > *sweetness*
> matched with
> > *matched with*
> guile
> > *guile*

I think the answer is largely a musical one. The constant interruption forces the reader to slow down and concentrate a little more on individual words as s/he reads, and there is a rhythmical pattern that is established in the second example that doesn't exist in the first. The musical term for such repetition is *heterophony*, "a type of texture characterized by the simultaneous variation of a single melodic line. Such a texture can be regarded as a kind of complex monophony in which there is only one basic melody, but realized at the same time in multiple voices . . ." (*Wikipedia*). It has seemed to me for some time now that one of the great insights of the twentieth century is the notion that *some parts of the mind don't know what other parts of the mind are doing*—that mind is multiple and by no means necessarily unified. How can an "I" represent that? I have "interrupted" other people's poems, as in this example from Charles Bukowski:

> the mockingbird had been following the cat
> all summer
> mocking mocking mocking

which became in my version

> the mockingbird had been following the cat
> *there was this cat*
> all summer

and I only saw him
mocking mocking mocking
once

I have also written poems in which two voices—different but both scripted by me—intercept one another, sometimes speaking simultaneously.

In the poems in which I repeat lines exactly, as in "SHE IS IN MY LIFE!," I am trying to suggest the presence of an echo in the mind, of another area in which the words repeat and are perhaps changed. The words are not the utterance of an "I" as such but of something which echoes in different ways within. The fact that information is repeated but not for emphasis suggests that the conveying of information is not the only—not even necessarily the central—issue of the poem. These pieces can be performed solo but also with a second voice as the echo. It seems to me that our "individual" voices have the kind of being we have in general—that they are multiple and capable of many different kinds of sound. We say that a poet finds his (or her) "voice," but I think it would be more accurate to say that a poet finds his (or her) *voices*—or, perhaps better, as Diane di Prima once said, *that the voices find him/her.* For me, all this is a music, and the music is the primary thing. Words have meanings, yes, but in a poem they also have a musical quality. This music can be expressed in a myriad of different ways.

My work arises out of a confusion resulting from the conflicting needs to communicate clearly and to transcend communication entirely—to turn language into an instrument of transformation. This book is in a way an experiment in sound. My poems are all shillelagh songs.

PEOPLE WHO TELL YOU THAT POETRY

is essentially speech
do not mean that
poetry is essentially speech
they mean that
poetry is essentially speech
by one person
that the poem is the utterance
of the "individual"—
the undivided selfthey do not see speech
as multiple
do not follow
the many-voiced examples
of Whitman's
"Out of the Cradle Endlessly Rocking"
Eliot's
"The Waste Land"
Pound's

"Cantos"
do not see speech
as something that may be
opposed
to writing
as something
that writing cannot quite
capture
as something
in some senses freer
than writing: "winged" . . .
so that speech for them
leads back to text
leads back to page
and not to tongue talk
not to action
not to what I am doing
at this very moment
though you cannot hear it
though your ears strain
and your voice catches
and you believe
that I am
writing

Jack Foley has published 15 books of poetry, 5 books of criticism, a book of stories, and a two-volume, 3,000-page "chronoencyclopedia," *Visions & Affiliations: California Poetry 1940-2005*. He became well known through his multi-voiced performances with his late wife, Adelle, also a poet. He currently performs with his new life partner, Sangye Land. Since 1988 he has presented poetry on Berkeley radio station KPFA. He has received Lifetime Achievement Awards from Marquis Who's Who and the Berkeley Poetry Festival. June 5, 2010 was declared "Jack Foley Day" in Berkeley. His recent publications include *EYES* (selected poems); *The Tiger & Other Tales*, a book of stories; *Riverrun*, a book of experimental poetry; and *Grief Songs*, a book documenting his grief at the death of his wife.